The Astute Private Investor

D1350284

About the Author

Kevin Goldstein-Jackson is a successful private investor – in good times and bad.

In the *Financial Times* he wrote (1st August 1987) about his 'Fear of the Crash' and, on 17th October 1987, he described how he had started selling in July and had increased his selling in September as he anticipated 'sharp declines'. On 19th October 1987 in New York the Dow Jones share index plummeted 508 points and, in London, the FT-SE 100 share index fell 250 points.

Interviewed on Bloomberg TV on Saturday 10th March 2001 about the state of the Stock Market, he said: "I think there is going to be a further shake out in America . . ." On Monday 12th March, Wall Street plunged and by the end of that week the Dow Jones Index had fallen by 821 points – its biggest weekly loss since 1989.

The Astute Private Investor will help *you* decide which shares to buy – when to sell – and shows how to beat the professionals at their own game.

Can *you* afford not to read this book?

The Astute Private Investor

A share-picker's guide

by

Kevin Goldstein-Jackson

RIGHT WAY
plus

Investing in shares carries an element of risk and the values of shares and dividends can fall as well as rise. Financial trends, conditions, regulations and other matters affecting trading in shares are subject to change. This book is sold with the understanding that the Author and Publishers are not engaged in providing any particular share recommendations, legal, accounting or other professional service, and that there is no actual or implied contract, professional or business relationship between the Author and reader, and that the Author and Publishers accept no responsibility whatsoever for any actions carried out by the reader or readers as a result of reading all or part of this book.

The Astute Private Investor provides general information to the private investor. The Author regrets that he is not able to reply to any correspondence nor recommend or comment on any specific named shares. For such advice the opinions of a stockbroker or other reputable professional financial adviser should be sought.

Typeset in 11/13½ pt Legacy Serif Book by Letterpart Ltd., Reigate, Surrey.
Printed and bound in Great Britain by Guernsey Press Co. Ltd., Guernsey, Channel Islands.

The *Right Way Plus* series is published by Elliot Right Way Books, Brighton Road, Lower Kingswood, Tadworth, Surrey, KT20 6TD, U.K. For information about our company and the other books we publish, visit our web site at www.right-way.co.uk

Contents

Dedication and Acknowledgements

THE ASTUTE PRIVATE INVESTOR is dedicated with many thanks and much appreciation to John Edwards, former Personal Finance Editor of the *Financial Times*, for first encouraging me to write about some of my investment experiences for that newspaper.

This book is also dedicated to my wife, Mei Leng; and to my two daughters: Sing Yu, who kindly double-checked the proofs, and Kimberley, who provided me with delicious home-made ginger biscuits.

I would also like to express my grateful thanks to Malcolm Purvis of Nielson Cobbold stockbrokers for reading drafts of *THE ASTUTE PRIVATE INVESTOR* and for all his extremely helpful comments and suggestions.

I am also most grateful to Stuart Goldsmith, Chairman of Ketton Investments, and Jeremy Lewis of Butterfield Securities for their very helpful comments and suggestions on the earlier version.

However, all opinions expressed in *THE ASTURE PRIVATE INVESTOR* are mine and should not be taken to imply that they or their firms agree with them.

I would also like to thank Malcolm and Clive Elliot for all their most valuable encouragement, comments, criticism and assistance.

Introduction

'Playing the Stock Market is easy. I make well over seventy-five thousand a year by it: it's better than working.'

'Shares are risky. What if I lose all my money?'

'I don't know anything about shares. I prefer to leave that sort of thing to the professionals.'

Three different investment views: there are many more. Yet investing on the Stock Market can be profitable, interesting and fun – *and* it is possible to beat some of the professionals.

To be a successful investor you do *not* need to learn lots of technical terms and investment theories, nor do you need a great deal of money to start.

Many investment theories do not work in practice, and much of the technical jargon appears to be designed either as an 'imposing' or 'shortened' way to express simple ideas. Chapter Two on *The Basics* explains some of the more useful technical terms.

When I first began buying shares I only had £150 to invest. Now I deal in many thousands and decide the investments in my own personal pension scheme. This book has drawn on some of my own investment experiences as a private investor. I do not claim to be infallible. Some of my share purchases have resulted in losses, but at least such losses have taught me some of the pitfalls of investment.

Some of my investments in shares have produced gains of over 100% within 12 months of their purchase dates. Others have performed remarkably well over a longer period.

Of course, not all my investments have fared so well, but over the years the profits have been considerably more than the losses. Even in 1987, the 'year of the Crash', I still made money.

The Astute Private Investor is only concerned with buying shares directly. It does not deal with unit trusts, currency funds and Government stock – nor does it deal with traded options. The aim was to produce a book that was of a manageable length and was fairly easy to understand. Traded options can be a complex subject, and to provide proper details of how to profit from them would require a separate book – especially as options can be highly speculative, and it is possible to lose all your investment. In my view it is somewhat easier and safer to make money from direct ownership of shares than in traded options.

The book is also designed to be 'fairly undatable' to avoid the necessity of revising and reprinting it every time there is a change in tax legislation. It also saves the reader from having to buy a new edition of this book every year. Therefore, for tax advice on the suitability of investments, please consult your accountant, stockbroker, bank manager or other financial adviser.

The Astute Private Investor does not name specific shares which should be purchased: any such 'share tips' would have been out-of-date within weeks of the book being published. What the book does try to do, however, is to give some general guidance as to how to make money on the Stock Market.

Finally, parts of this book are opinionated. Some people, no doubt, will disagree with certain of my views which tend to be rather cynical: but at least such views have enabled me to prosper from my investments.

Hopefully, *The Astute Private Investor* will be of interest as much to the experienced investor as to the beginner.

Happy investing!

KG-J

Chapter 1:

Why It's Possible To Beat Some Of The Professionals

Loss-Making Investments

Suppose you invested £1,000 and, after five years, found that the value of your investment had fallen to less than £800. You would not be very pleased.

You might also be rather disappointed if an investment of £10,000 shrank to be worth less than £9,000 after just twelve months.

With investment performances like these, you might well decide to give up buying shares directly and let the professionals handle your spare cash instead. Yet the two examples given here *were* the performance results of professionals!

Unit Trust Performance

Many unit trusts are very keen to boast of their performance – *if they do well*. Yet if you look at performance tables for various unit trusts you will find that some of them have produced a mediocre performance – while others have actually *lost* a sizeable percentage of their investors' money.

Of course, some unit trusts have produced a reasonable performance and some have made excellent returns for their investors over both the short and long term.

However, the problem with unit trusts is that there are well over 1,000 of them and it is difficult to decide which will perform the best. Many of them are highly specialized – only investing in, for example, Japanese or American or European companies, or businesses in 'emerging markets' or companies involved in gold or property or some other particular area of activity.

The investor therefore has to think very carefully before investing his money: will the gold price rise or fall? Will there be political problems in Japan – or in some of the 'emerging countries'? All sorts of things have to be considered.

A cynic might think that one of the reasons why some fund managers have created so many different unit trusts is so that they are more likely to have something to boast about and promote.

X TRUST – NUMBER ONE BEST PERFORMANCE TRUST IN ITS SECTOR

Yet for how long will it remain number one? Is it in a sector that has large swings between high and low share prices? How well (or badly) did other unit trusts run by the same management group perform?

If one trust performs very badly, then the management group can easily stop advertising it and promote, instead, one of its better-performing trusts, thus still keeping the name of the management group in the public eye.

The managers can also hope that when the poor investor sees his investment in a particular unit trust perform badly, he will blame himself for not investing in a different unit trust run by the same group, rather than wishing he had never invested with the management group at all.

However, unit trust management groups can equally

point out that 'league tables' of all their trusts' performances are published regularly, so that any management
group which has a consistent record of poor performance
can easily be spotted and avoided.

The more unit trusts there are, the greater the choice for
the individual investor. An investor might believe, for example, that US companies will outperform European ones over
the next five years and so would not be attracted to a more
general trust that invested in European *and* US companies.
The investor may well be wrong, but at least he had a choice.
The specialization of unit trusts is therefore simply a
response to demands from investors for a wider choice of
trusts.

Average Performance

But the *average* performance of unit trust managers is
hardly inspiring. Many of them fail to perform as well as the
FT-SE Actuaries All Share Index. This means that when you
read newspaper reports that the Stock Market has gone up
by a certain percentage, many unit trust fund managers will
not have achieved even that percentage increase for their
fund, let alone beaten the Index. Similarly, if the Index has
fallen, the value of an investor's holding in a unit trust may
have fallen even further.

I could quote all sorts of statistics as evidence for this, but
sceptics might say: 'Well, this was true when he was writing
the book, but I've seen lots of publicity about how well unit
trusts have performed, so his figures are all out-of-date and
unit trusts are all now performing wonderfully well.'

So, if anyone doubts my statements regarding the performance of some unit trusts, then a visit to the local library with a
request to look at the latest publication giving performance
details for unit trusts could well produce surprising results.

There is a huge difference between the best and worst performing funds. Back the right one and you could make lots of money. Pick the wrong one and you may lose quite a bit of your investment.

Fund Managers' Results

The performance of the average mutual fund manager in the US is often equally uninspiring – and the same is true of many fund managers in other countries.

Even some of the managers of pension and life assurance funds fail to produce other than a mediocre performance although some, of course, produce sparkling results.

Just because a fund is run by professionals does not automatically mean its results will be good: professional performance varies.

The Problems of the Professionals: Size

Why does the average professionally run fund perform so badly? Is such poor performance an indication that an individual private investor can do better?

The problem with fund managers is that they operate under a number of handicaps which do not affect the ordinary private investor.

Suppose a private investor believes the Stock Market has risen too much and is due for a sharp fall. He can sell all his shares and sit back happily with cash in the bank. Few fund managers either can or will do that. Specialization has its problems. If a unit trust promotes itself as investing only in American companies or Australian companies or any other sort of company, then that is what it must do with the bulk of its funds. It cannot sell *all* its shareholdings and sit on a pile of cash for a year or more.

Even general funds and pension funds have problems, simply because many of them are so large. Suppose an individual investor has a shareholding of, say, £1,000 or even £25,000 in a large company and sells it. In terms of the size of that company, his shareholding was tiny and so his sale will not cause the share price of the company to fall.

It takes lots of small sellers to make the share prices of large companies fall. Together, ten thousand private investors might well own considerably less than 1% of a large company. But one pension fund might well own by itself 2% or more of a large company. If it sells the shares all at the same time, then unless there is a very eager buyer – perhaps another pension fund or possibly a take-over bidder – the share price of that company will probably fall. If few people want something, then usually the price drops in order to tempt a buyer.

Fund Following

Fund managers also 'keep an eye' on each other. If one fund manager sells a large number of shares in a particular company, then other fund managers may well start asking: 'What does fund manager X know about that company? Is it going to report lower profits?' If two or more fund managers sell their large shareholdings in the same company within days of each other, then some other fund managers might well sell out too. Many large companies have considerably more than 50% of their shares held by fund managers and other institutional investors. In many cases, the fund managers *are* the market: what they do with their investment funds affects everyone else.

If the majority of the fund managers decide to buy, then share prices will probably go up. If the biggest fund managers sell, then the market will go down.

It is interesting to reflect on the fact that on 'Black Monday' (19th October 1987) when the Dow Jones share index fell 508 points, just fifteen fund managers/ institutions accounted for about 20% of all the shares sold in New York on that day. Suppose they had bought instead of sold?

The more big sellers, the lower the prices of the shares being sold and, if few – if any – people buy, then prices can plummet.

Forced Sellers

Unit trusts in the UK, and certain types of mutual funds in the US, can sometimes be forced sellers of shares – even if the fund managers concerned may wish to *buy* shares instead.

For example, suppose the government suddenly announced a new, very tax advantageous investment opportunity. This could cause some people to sell a number of their holdings in unit trusts in order to have funds available for the new investment.

Fashions change. Investors may decide they no longer find a particular sector attractive, so they may sell their holdings in a trust specialising in that sector in order to invest in a trust involved in a completely different sector. Investors might also sell their holdings in a trust managed by a particular company in order to invest in a trust run by another company whose performance they think will be better; or they may wish to sell their unit trust holdings because they are fearful of another Stock Market crash.

In order to pay cash to investors selling their units, the unit trust managers will have to utilize the cash resources of the fund, attract new investors to the fund, or sell some of the investments held by the fund.

If the fund is not proving attractive to new investors, and if it has limited cash available and if there are many investors wanting to sell their holdings, then the fund will be forced to sell certain of its investments in order to pay those departing investors.

The fund managers may feel that they have invested in shares in companies that will perform remarkably well – but they may have to sell some of those shares to raise cash. The more they have to sell then, in the absence of any strong buying interest for those shares, the greater will be the fall in the price of the shares.

Perhaps the market has gone into a steep decline and the fund managers feel that now is the right time to 'bottom pick' – choosing shares that are currently depressed but which, over time, will outperform many others. The fund managers may not be able to buy such 'bargains' because they have no spare cash available – all the cash is going to pay investors selling their units in the fund.

A private investor does not suffer from such constraints. No one is beating on his door demanding money from investments and forcing him even to sell shares in high quality companies and/or miss any 'bargain' opportunities.

Small Companies

Size also counts against the fund managers in the type of investment they can make. They have millions and millions of pension fund, insurance, unit trust, etc., money flowing into them every day. That money has to be invested. But where?

Some years ago, when I was Chief Executive of a UK public quoted company (of which I was also the founder), various pension fund managers were invited to 'pitch' for running the company's pension scheme.

I asked each of them: 'Do you invest in small companies?'

Two of them said they did. 'How "small" is "small"?' I asked.

'Twenty million,' replied one of the fund managers.

I responded: 'My company is worth less than twenty million. I think the share price will double within two years. Yet your fund will not invest in it, nor in any other enterprising company unless it is valued at twenty million or more. You must be missing out on hundreds of successful companies.'

That fund manager did not get to manage my company's pension fund. They probably stuck yet more money into big Blue-Chip companies where the share price hardly moved, and in other large companies which may have performed better but still did not match my own company's share price which rose by over 50% in that year.

So why do so many fund managers ignore 'small' companies? (And if 'small' to them is twenty million, one wonders why some of them – who happen to be in the insurance business – quibble about paying out promptly on claims worth a few thousand.)

One of the reasons for certain fund managers' lack of investment in small companies is due to the impossibility of actually acquiring shares in some small companies at a reasonable price. With all the millions flowing into its coffers, the fund management company wants to make investments of a reasonable size.

An investment of £100,000 in a company worth a billion will probably be fairly easy to make: there may be many millions of shares in the company available.

An investment of £100,000 in a company worth, say, £7 million, may prove difficult. The directors of the company may own half of it and be unwilling to sell any shares. Possibly 15% of the rest might be owned by a number of venture capital funds which made their investment when the company first started and they, too, do not want to sell at present: they feel the company still has great potential. Most of the other shareholders are also not keen on selling: perhaps they like the company's products, its management, its future prospects.

Thus, to make an investment of £100,000 the fund manager might have to offer considerably more than the current share price in order to persuade sufficient owners of shares to sell them to his fund. This might then leave the fund manager as the largest single shareholder (excluding directors) in the company. If at some future date he wishes to sell the shares he worries that he might not be able to find a buyer at any price, let alone the price he originally paid for his investment. Therefore, he avoids investing in small companies.

Even if he did invest £100,000 in a small company, as his fund may be worth well over £1 billion, the fact that his £100,000 small company investment doubled in six months, or went up 350% in three years, is unlikely to affect the overall performance of his fund: it is a tiny drop in his ocean.

The fund manager also has to keep track of all his investments. Dividends have to be properly credited, share performances monitored, annual reports and company statements read. It takes an awful lot of £50,000 and £100,000 investments to 'dispose' of a billion or more: no wonder so many fund managers prefer to invest individual sums of £250,000 or £500,000 or £1 million or more only in large companies.

Thus, the private investor has the great advantage of being able to invest in small companies at a reasonable price. His £1,000 or £10,000 or even £20,000 or more investment should still be able to find a choice of attractive companies where such an investment will not unduly affect the share price.

League Tables

Another disadvantage for the fund manager is that what he does is open to public inspection – or at least to the trustees of the funds he manages. Suppose he makes a mistake? He believes a Stock Market crash is about to happen, sells 20% of his fund's entire share portfolio – and then the market rises and keeps on rising and the crash doesn't happen. Will his employers still want him? Will people still invest in his fund?

If a private investor made the same mistake, no one need know about it – except the investor's stockbroker – and if the investor uses two different stockbroking firms, then even they need not necessarily know he's missed out on a booming market: one broker might think the investor has just given more of his business to the other broker.

The fund manager is expected to perform. League tables are published comparing his performance with that of other fund managers. How has *his* fund performed each quarter?

Suppose an international fund manager thinks that Australian shares are likely to outperform shares elsewhere in the world. He puts 15% of his fund's assets in Australian companies. There is then a slump in shares in Australia and share prices fall by more than 25%. What has that done to the performance of his fund compared to the performance of others whose fund managers did not invest so much in Australia?

If, at the end of a year, a fund has remained static – or even gone down in value while most of the other funds have gone up – then the fund manager might be in some fear for his job or, at least, concerned about the future levels of his salary and bonuses. This makes many fund managers either 'play safe' or try for short-term gains.

Chasing short-term gains can lead to buying and selling shares very rapidly. In the US, some fund managers 'turn over' their entire share portfolios more than once in a single year: not one share do they hold for more than twelve months. Yet some of them produce worse results than if they had remained a whole year with exactly the same shares as they had held at the start of the year.

In the UK, fund managers have become increasingly prepared to change the shares in their portfolios – especially if they are operating highly visible funds, such as unit trusts, which are in open competition with other funds for investors' money.

At one time, pension fund management was regarded as fairly stable: whichever company was appointed to manage a particular firm's pension scheme remained working for that firm, through good times and bad.

Now, many firms have regular 'beauty parades' when representatives from a number of fund management companies have to 'pitch' for the right to manage the firm's pension fund while the existing manager of the fund has to try to justify why his company should continue to manage the fund.

Will the pension fund trustees be attracted to what appears to them to be a more energetic fund manager? Will the trustees accept that the downturn in their fund's value over the past year was due to the fund manager adopting a strategy that will pay off in a major way over the longer term? Will the trustees switch the fund's management to a manager whose performance has recently been much better over the shorter term?

Many fund managers have to worry over the short-term

performance of their funds and how they compare with their rivals.

The private investor does not have to bother with quarterly 'league tables' for his own share performances. If he buys shares in a company he believes in and the share price doesn't move for a year, then he is under little pressure to sell: maybe his patience will be rewarded and the share price will soar the following year. No one will fire him because his shareholdings did not increase in value over 12 months, nor will anything happen to him if, the following year, they only rise by 5%. Maybe they will rise 100% in year three. He can take a longer-term view than many fund managers.

Index Following

The 'league tables' of funds' performances also encourage large numbers of fund managers to 'play safe'. They manage an 'indexed fund'.

Perhaps they might only buy shares in the companies that make up the FT-SE 100 share index (the 'Footsie' index): their buying will be restricted to shares in the 100 companies in that index – generally, the largest UK public quoted companies. Or they may invest only in shares in one of the other share indices.

This happens even more in the US, where many fund managers follow Standard & Poor's 500 share index (the S & P 500) and only buy shares in those 500 companies included in that index.

The fund manager of an 'indexed' fund may well carry out considerable readjustments in the size of its investment in each company in order to try to reflect its 'weighting' in the index concerned. If a company is 'dropped' from an index and replaced by another, then the fund manager 'tracking' that index will have to do the same. (See also 'Index Changes' in Chapter 3, *What To Look For In A Share* on pages 83-84.)

If the market rises, then obviously many of the companies included in the index will rise, too, and so the funds that invest in those companies will also rise.

If, of course, the market plummets, then the indexed funds plummet too, but at least the fund managers can say to their clients: 'Well, we didn't perform worse than the index.' And it does look nice on a chart: the performance of a fund not going below the line of that of the market index.

A private investor can ignore the index. He is unlikely to have sufficient funds to invest directly in 100 or more companies anyway. He needn't 'play safe'. He can seek out those companies which have better than average prospects – some that are not in any 100- or 500-share index.

The private investor can also avoid investing in some badly managed companies that *are* included in some of these indices simply because the companies concerned are so large. Just because a company is big doesn't mean it will keep getting bigger or keep making profits or prevent its share price from falling.

Backing Hunches

The private investor can 'back a hunch': he does not have to justify his investment decisions to anyone except himself and possibly his immediate family. If he feels a small company will prosper – but not many people have heard of it (like some of the computer software companies in their early days) – then he can invest in it. Some fund managers are not allowed to take such risks, even though the rewards might be considerable.

If a medium-size company has fallen on hard times, has

reported large losses and its shares are at an all-time low, then the private investor might decide to take a gamble and buy some of its shares in the hope that the company will be taken-over and 'sorted out' in such a way that its share price will rise dramatically.

A fund manager may take a similar view – but he might well risk far less than 1% of his fund in such a prospect, whereas a private investor might gamble 10% of his investment assets. If they are both right, and the shares do zoom upwards, the effect on the private investor's share portfolio will be considerably greater than that on the fund manager's fund.

Weighting And Other 'Rules'

Some fund managers have to worry about 'weighting' and other rules which affect their investment decisions.

For example, a number of fund managers have to follow complex 'rule books' which state what shares they can and cannot buy. One of the 'rules' might be that if general retailers make up X% of the value of all the shares quoted on the Stock Market, then the fund has to put X% or even X% plus Y% of its assets in the general retail sector. If one company accounts for, say 3% of the value of that sector, then the fund, too, would have to be 'weighted' to take account of this. However, this need not mean the fund putting 3% of its fund set aside for retail company shares into that company, as the fund may well not want to buy shares in every general retail company but just, say, the largest five. The fund manager will then have to work out exactly what percentage of his funds for retail investment have to be placed in shares of each of the five general retailers.

The prospect of an imminent drop in consumer demand,

or an approaching market crash, would not necessarily deter certain fund managers from going ahead with such investments – simply because it stated in the 'rule book' that they *had* to invest.

The private investor can ignore such nonsense and only invest in general retail shares (or any other shares) when he believes the share price may be about to rise.

Following The Herd

As mentioned earlier, the average fund manager is interested in what other fund managers are doing. If several fund managers suddenly start increasing their shareholdings in, say, electrical goods retailers, then others may also feel that they, too, have to invest in the electrical goods sector.

Maybe they are all wrong. Perhaps the share prices of electrical goods retailers will fall while other shares rise. But at least each fund manager concerned can point a finger at another fund manager and say to his bosses, trustees and clients, 'He did it too' – and thus attempt to mitigate the blame.

The private investor is under no obligation to 'follow the herd' (or, if it goes wrong, 'follow the nerd').

He will not 'lose face' if he makes a mistake – and he can always boast to his friends if he gets it right. His investment decisions can be purely his own personal choice uninfluenced by what many other people may be doing.

Committee Decisions

Some fund managers, before they can make a really major share purchase or change their investment strategy, have to persuade a committee or board of management that what they propose to do is justified. A private investor has no committee to answer to – he can therefore make major investment decisions much more quickly than a number of fund managers.

They Are The Market

There are many other advantages the private investor has over an average fund manager, but I hope that the ones outlined so far will have convinced you that it *is* possible to beat some of the professionals.

The fund managers and institutional investors cannot *all* beat the market – they are so large and control such vast shareholdings that, in many cases, they *are* the market.

Professional Advantages

The private investor should *not* completely ignore the possibilities of investing in unit trusts, entrusting his pension to a life assurance company or entrusting *some* of his savings to a fund manager. There are many fund managers who *do* produce excellent results – some far better than the average private investor could achieve, and sometimes there are significant tax advantages of 'investing with the professionals'.

The fund manager – because of the size of his investments – can obtain lower stockbroking fees than the average private investor. The larger the deal, the lower the percentage brokers' fee.

The private investor cannot get a very 'wide spread' of investments, mainly because he cannot afford directly to invest in a hundred or more different companies. A fund manager *can* achieve such a wide spread of investments because he has much greater funds available. However, it is probably easier to find, say, ten shares that are likely to outperform the average than it is to find one hundred, so a widely spread fund may find it somewhat more difficult to beat a fund or private investor with a much more limited share portfolio.

The private investor may well find it difficult to invest successfully in, say, Japanese companies. How will he find out their track record? How will he read some of their company reports? Some fund managers can do all that very well.

Unlike the private investor, a fund manager can make large direct investments in property – although a cynic might say that one of the reasons that some fund managers increased their property shareholdings after the 'Crash of '87' was because property values of giant office blocks, shopping centres, etc., are decided by comparatively few people since the market for them is limited. If fund managers decide not to sell them, then who is to say what those properties are really worth every three months or so?

Investors can look at newspapers and see the value of shares every day: they can see, for example, that a particular share has fallen by 5p in a day. But where do they read a daily value of a particular office block? So what does the ownership of office blocks, shopping centres, industrial buildings, etc., do for a fund's quarterly published investment performance?

However, the direct ownership of property can often bring considerable – and genuine – financial rewards.

Crash!

One of the factors that enabled me correctly to predict the 'Crash of '87' was the feeling that some financial institutions were playing 'pass the parcel' with shares.

They bought certain shares on Monday, sold them to another institution on Tuesday or Wednesday at a slightly higher price, that institution in turn sold them to another a day or so later, and so on. They were all making money.

The average investor could not have afforded to have bought, say, a million shares in a company for 105p and sold them for 106½p the following day. Turnover on world stock markets had shot up, largely because of institutions playing 'pass the parcel' – but what would happen if no one wanted to keep the parcel when the music stopped? I therefore sold many of my shares before the Crash. A lot of fund managers were 'caught out'.

Unlike the average private investor, the fund manager can afford to employ analysts and researchers and economists to try to find the best shares to buy – although the hefty salaries and 'perks' of such staff and the cost of their expensive office space might also give the funds considerable overheads. Even with the benefit of all this advice and research, some fund managers were still, just before the Crash, buying shares at very high prices and saying things like: 'We expect the market to keep rising until at least the middle of next year' and 'We are unlikely to see any serious setbacks in the market.' They lost a lot of money.

In the Introduction to this book I stated that it 'does not deal with unit trusts'. Yet this chapter has been full of references to unit trust and other fund managers. But *The Astute Private Investor* will not help you decide which unit trusts to buy. There are certainly some excellent trusts available: but it is outside the scope of this book to help you find them. The same is true of life assurance, pension fund and other managed fund investments: there are many excellent companies that are well run and which do product excellent results. So I repeat: do not overlook such investments.

Beat the 'Average Guys'

Although some fund managers are very good, we have also seen that the performance of many fund managers – the *average* fund manager – is rather pitiful.

You *could* beat these average guys because:

1. **You can sell all your shares if you think a crash is coming and sit on a pile of cash – many of them can't do this.**
2. **You can make decisions in private, you don't have to worry about 'losing face', or your position in a 'performance table' – many of them *do* have such worries and it can adversely affect their investment strategies.**
3. **You can invest in really small companies – many of them cannot.**
4. **You do not have to follow a 'rule book', an index, or consult a committee before you invest – your investment decisions can be much quicker and freer from restraints than many of theirs: and some of those restraints may well seriously affect their investment performance.**
5. **You're smart because you bought this book.**

It *is* possible to beat the average fund manager, but to do this you have to make many more investment decisions yourself. How will you make those decisions?

What follows is designed to assist in 'share picking'. And here I should also apologise for having so far (and throughout the rest of this book) referred to the private investor as 'he'. In fact, there are more women shareholders than men, so perhaps I should have used 'she' instead: no 'male chauvinist piggery' is intended.

Chapter 2:

The Basics

The experienced investor can skip this chapter.

What Sort Of An Investor Are You?

The answer to a question like that might be: 'I'm an investor who wants to make as much money as possible in the shortest possible time and with the minimum amount of risk.' Very good. But how are you going to do that?

Do you know exactly what sort of risks you are taking when you invest?

Would you believe everything a friend/newspaper journalist/company chairman/stockbroker/bank manager/financial adviser said about a company?

How long are you prepared to wait for an investment to rise? Would you panic and sell shares in a company if its share price plunged, say, 15 per cent in one day?

How much money can you afford to invest? How much can you afford to lose? Are you willing to invest money you have borrowed?

How much time can you devote to investment matters? Do you have time to follow closely the shares of a number of companies?

All these questions you need to ask yourself.

Investment Tests

If you are unsure as to how you would respond to the questions just raised, then – if you have not already invested on the Stock Market before – choose a few shares. Write down the name of each chosen company and its share price and the date you chose it. Decide how much you think you can afford to invest in each share (maybe you've only chosen one share or perhaps as many as ten) and write this down, too. **Do not buy the shares.**

Now look at the financial pages of your newspaper every day for three months – still *without buying* the shares. Have you read anything that would make you want to 'sell' those chosen shares? If so, write down the date when you would have 'sold' them and the reasons why, and the price at that time.

Have you read anything about any other shares you think you ought to buy? Write down the details, including the date you would have 'bought' them and the share price.

After *three months* of doing this, look at the results and consider them carefully. Did your chosen shares rise in price? Did you decide the market was 'too high' and not 'buy' anything at all?

Did you 'sell' a share which then went on to rise much higher, or plummet like a falling stone? Very few (if any) people ever manage to buy shares at their lowest point and sell them at their very highest. Even the best investors are always at least a few pence away from the 'low' and 'high' points when they buy and sell.

What has your three-month 'experiment' taught you about yourself?

Are you a 'natural gambler' who put his entire 'investment' in one highly speculative share or in a number of speculative shares which you also perhaps 'bought' and 'sold' quite rapidly?

Are you a 'cautious investor'? You put 'money' into 'safe' shares in well-known companies and 'sold' them when the price dropped a few pence, or perhaps you kept them when they did not move at all or only went up a few pence.

Are you a 'leave it to mature' investor? You 'bought' some shares and then just looked at their price occasionally: you were not too concerned if they went up or down over the three-month period as it was longer-term performance you were mostly interested in – or perhaps you only had time available to look at the share prices maybe once a week or less.

Are you an 'all-or-nothing' investor? You only 'bought' one or two shares. If they went up, you 'kept' them; if they went down a bit you 'sold' them and kept the 'cash'.

Are you an 'income seeking' investor? You mainly 'bought' shares because their dividend payments were quite good and you welcomed this 'income'.

Are you a 'worrier investor'? You worried you might have picked the 'wrong' shares; you worried every time they went down slightly; you worried when they went up and did not 'sell' them and take a quick 'profit'; you worried when the share price did not move at all.

Are you a 'balanced investor'? You carefully thought about what you wanted from your investments – a bit of long-term growth, some speculative short-term profits, and reasonable dividend income.

Are you an 'I can only afford to invest in one company' investor? – so you 'invested' in the shares of one company and hoped that you would be able to make a 'profit'.

It does not matter what sort of investor you are, unless you are the 'worrier' sort; nor does it matter whether the 'performance' of your chosen shares over the three-month period was good or bad: a closer study of this book should help you with your 'share picking' when you 'do it for real'.

The only people who might still have major problems are the 'worrier investors'. Worrying over the performance (or non-performance) of your shares can lead you to make wrong decisions and might produce ulcers (or even lead to a heart attack). Perhaps 'worrier investors' shouldn't be investing in shares at all? But then, where else will they put their 'spare cash'? If they put it in a bank they will probably worry that inflation will 'eat away' the value of their capital. If they put it in a fund manager's hands they'll worry that they've chosen the wrong fund manager. If they spend it all they'll worry that they won't have enough to live on when they retire/get older. Perhaps they can try not to worry so much?

Affordable Investing

Whatever type of investor you are, it is probably best for beginners to invest in shares only the money they can afford to lose. I know it gives me 'pain' whenever I lose money on a particular share deal – but any losses I make I can afford. They could not cause me any real grief.

My profits from share dealing have always been considerably more than my losses – but I still take the view that one year the situation might change. It seldom pays to be over-confident in your own ability.

Any investor who claims *never* to have made a loss on a share deal is possibly one or more of the following:

(a) Someone who never made a share deal or has only dealt on a comparatively few occasions.
(b) Someone who only dealt for a fairly short time – all of it during a booming Stock Market.
(c) Someone using illegal 'insider' information.
(d) A liar.

(e)   Someone only dealing in shares in his own company or associated companies; or someone who missed out on a lot of good deals in favour of a more pedestrian performance.

I have never borrowed money to buy shares – I've always saved up until I could afford to buy them. It helps that I've never smoked: what one person might spend on cigarettes a year makes an ideal starting 'cash pile'.

Sometimes I've cancelled plans for an overseas holiday or to buy a new car simply so I can use that spare cash to buy more shares instead. This is usually to take advantage of a 'special situation': buying shares in a company I've suddenly realized might be a take-over target, or a company that might announce excellent profits which most people were not expecting, or a company that might benefit from suddenly changing circumstances – like sudden mass demand for its products. If such a share soars I take some profits and go on an even better holiday!

Some people *do* make a fortune buying shares with borrowed money. I think it's too risky.

Some people maintain that you should have a 'wide spread' of investments. But if you've only got, say, £500 to start with, then that's impossible unless you put it in a unit trust or similar fund. If you really can only spare £500, then I think it's better if you just buy shares in one company: one you really believe in and know something about. Your £500 investment may only be worth £450 (or less) at the end of a year but, maybe, it might rise to £750 or more in eighteen months or so. I have experienced seeing a £500 investment increase to £4,500 in less than eighteen months. You might even do better than that or you might lose half your original investment. But at least you will have made your own investment decisions and will learn from experience: future investments might do better.

What Is A Share?

This may seem a rather silly question, but it is still worth asking. A share is a share in a company. If a company has, say, 1,000,000 issued shares and you buy 1,000 of them then you own one-thousandth of the entire company. You are one of the company's owners. Whatever the directors and management may think, they are answerable for their actions to their company's owners: its shareholders.

But there are different types of share, and each UK share has a *nominal value* which is also known as its *par value*. It is not unusual to pay £1 or more for a share that has a nominal value of only 5p per share. You are not being 'cheated' out of 95p per share.

The nominal value is simply the 'value' a company puts on its shares. Even when a company is privatized or first comes to the Stock Market, its nominal value per share may be far less than it is asking investors to pay for them.

Why have a nominal value at all if it is so meaningless in relation to a share's actual value? Indeed, in some other countries, shares can have no par value at all. But in the UK, under company law, each company must set a par value on its ordinary shares. What the par value is, and why it is what it is for each company, is a matter best left to accountants and lawyers. It doesn't much affect you as an investor.

The most widely bought shares are called *ordinary shares*. These can be *voting shares*, which give their holders the right to vote at the company's annual general meeting and can be useful in helping to decide whether or not a take-over bid should be accepted or whether or not a director should be re-appointed.

Some companies also have *non-voting* shares which do not give their holders the right to a vote, but otherwise the holders still own a part of the company.

Usually, voting shares cost more to buy than non-voting shares simply because if someone wants to take-over the company he is more likely to be interested in acquiring a reasonable holding of voting shares before he launches his bid.

A small number of companies have *A shares* and *B shares*. The *A* shares may have different voting rights from the *B* shares. For example, it may be that the *A* shares have no voting rights at all: a shareholder with such shares would be unable to vote for or against the re-election of directors or any other motion put before a Meeting of the Company. It might, instead, be that the *A* shares carry one vote per share and, in certain circumstances, that each *B* share might have, say, five votes.

One would think that if there are *ordinary shares* then there must also be *extraordinary shares*. In a way, there are such shares but they are called *preference* rather than *extraordinary shares*. These shares carry the right to a dividend, which is usually fixed. If the company falls on hard times, then the preference shareholders are supposed to be treated to their dividend before the ordinary shareholders: indeed, there may not be sufficient funds to pay the ordinary shareholders a dividend at all. Some preference shares are 'cumulative' which means that if a dividend has been missed in the past (perhaps because the company fell on hard times) then there is a right for that dividend to be paid in arrears the following year, or perhaps even later, when circumstances permit. Sometimes the preference shares have a 'convertible' option – under certain conditions, the preference shares can be converted into ordinary shares.

Partly-paid shares are what their name implies: only part of the payment for them has been paid. More money still needs to be paid for them, normally by a specified date.

Warrants may be given by some companies to holders of certain types of its shares. The warrants may entitle the holders of them to buy a certain number of shares in the company at a certain price by a specified date. Warrants can usually be traded in their own right.

A *scrip issue* is also known as a *bonus issue* or a *capitalization issue*. This is where a company issues a certain number of new shares, free, to its existing shareholders in proportion to their current shareholding in the company.

For example, a company's shares are, say, £10 each.

The company has a one-for-one scrip issue: for each share an investor holds in that company, he is given one more share. Theoretically, the company concerned is worth no more than it was before the scrip issue: all it is doing is reducing its share price from £10 to 500p per share. The total value of an individual's shareholding is still the same: instead of holding, say, 500 shares worth £10 each (£5,000), after a one-for-one scrip issue he still holds his 500 original shares (which are now worth 500p each instead of £10) *plus* 500 new shares (worth 500p each) making a total shareholding of 1,000 shares worth 500p each (£5,000).

However, the price of a company's shares does not necessarily drop to half its previous level after a one-for-one scrip issue. Psychologically, some people are reluctant to buy what they think are 'highly priced' shares: they would prefer to own 1,000 shares at, perhaps, 510p each (£5,100) rather than 500 shares at £10 each (£5,000): so after a scrip issue you might find that more people have been attracted to the shares. This increased buying makes the share price rise and so the value of your shareholding *has* increased.

Sometimes, before a scrip issue, a company might state

that it 'hopes' or 'expects' to 'maintain the dividend' on the new shares. This is good news. For example, if the dividend paid on each of the original 500 shares was, say, 15p per share (£75 in total) then the company hopes to pay at least the same 15p per share dividend on the increased number of shares. As you now have 1,000 shares instead of the original 500 you should now get at least £150 in dividends each year instead of £75. Such news should also help to make the price of the shares go up.

A scrip issue need not be on a one-for-one basis. It might be offered as a one-for-three or one-for-five or on some other basis instead.

Share splits are much the same as bonus issues, except that instead of 'increasing its capital' (issuing more new shares) a company decides to split the value of each share. A share with, say, a nominal value of £1 (but which actually sells for, say, £10) might be 'split' (ie: divided) into five shares with a nominal value of 20p each (and which will actually sell for £2 each).

Rights issues happen when a company wants to raise money from its shareholders for expansion and other purposes. The company invites its existing shareholders to take up more shares in the company, normally at a lower price than the existing price of the shares. The existing shareholders have a *right* to apply for the new shares in proportion to their existing shareholding. A shareholder does *not* have to take up his rights entitlement if he does not want to (see also *A Right Worth Having?* page 131).

In addition to *quoted shares* (those quoted/listed on a Stock Exchange) it is also possible to use a stockbroker to buy and sell shares in certain *unquoted* companies. However, caution is especially needed when dealing with such investments as the risks are much greater than dealing in shares in companies with a full Stock Exchange quotation.

For example, while it may be quite easy to buy shares in

certain unquoted companies, it can sometimes be difficult to sell them because there may be few buyers of the shares and/or there is a wide difference between the buying price and the selling price of the shares.

How To Find A Stockbroker

The best way to find a stockbroker is from personal recommendation: do you know anyone who uses a stockbroker and who thinks highly of the firm concerned?

Publications like *The Investors Chronicle* regularly give details of brokers and their commissions, services offered, minimum size of investment required, etc.

You *don't* necessarily have to deal with the broker in your home town. Deals are usually done on the phone, not by letter or personal visit. I live in Dorset and deal with two excellent brokers: one in Southampton, Hampshire and the other in London. You could also deal with a broker 'on-line' via the internet.

If you feel happier dealing with someone 'face to face', then consider using the broker nearest to you, or use the services of your local bank or maybe there is a 'share shop' or a building society offering 'share services' near you, which you can use instead.

Do *not* use the services of anyone who phones you from abroad and who is not registered by the appropriate authorities.

You should also look carefully at the type of service offered by each broker. Some are only interested in clients with lots of money to invest – others are quite happy to act for people who just want to buy, say, £1,000 worth of shares every year or so.

There are a number of large London broking firms who 'look down their noses' at investors with less than £25,000 (some don't even want investors with less than £50,000). If you just have the minimum £25,000 or £50,000 to invest, then ignore these brokers as you still might run the risk of being 'dumped' if, after a year or so, they decide to raise their 'minimum limits' to perhaps £100,000. It is sometimes better to be a 'big fish' in a small pool than a minnow in an ocean: at least that way you get noticed and are less likely to be 'forgotten'.

Some people imagine that all London brokers are like double cream – rich and thick – getting large salaries and bonuses for poor advice and being interested in only dealing for very wealthy clients. This is *not* true. There are a number of small London firms providing an excellent service to people who only want to invest a few thousand pounds. They just hope such investors will do well and so will eventually have more to invest.

Brokers' Services

Some brokers will try to persuade you to use their 'discretionary services': the broker asks you about your investment objectives, and then *he* decides what to invest your money in. This has no appeal to me: I prefer to choose my own investments and make my own mistakes and have my own successes.

Before you actually approach a broker, make sure you know what you want from him. Do you want any advice? If not, you might well be financially better off using a broker who provides a 'deals only' service where his commission charges will probably be less than those of a broker who will provide advice on the merits (or otherwise) of certain shares.

If you are just starting out with investment in shares, then choose a broking firm that provides a 'deals only' service *and* a more comprehensive service that includes investment advice. You can start off using his more expensive service (the advisory service) and then later switch, depending on your experience (and the quality of his advice) to his 'deals only' service. (I prefer using the expression 'deals only' rather than the term used by brokers of 'execution only': execution somehow sounds rather ominous and final.) Some very experienced and successful investors use brokers' advisory services because they appreciate being able to use their brokers as a 'sounding board' for their own ideas and welcome any 'market gossip' or other useful information that the broker might give them.

Do you want to buy shares in foreign companies? If so, then there is little point in approaching a broker who has little experience or knowledge of dealing in such shares.

Do you want to do lots of fairly small deals rather than just a few large ones? If you do, then look carefully at the various levels of commission charged by different brokers. Some brokers have a rather high 'minimum charge' so that every small deal can be expensive; whereas other brokers have a lower minimum charge, but charge a higher percentage commission.

Do you want to use a broker's nominee services, where shares are held in the nominee name, rather than registered in your name? If so, then how much does this nominee service cost? How easy (and costly) will it be for the nominee to arrange for you to receive company reports from the companies in which you have invested? Would you consider being a sponsored member of Crest, the electronic share settlement system, where your broker acts as your sponsor, but the shares you buy are registered in your name and not that of a nominee? If so, ask the broker to send you a Crest handbook which explains the system in detail.

Do you want to make use of a broker's 'cash management account' or similar service where the broker holds your cash on deposit so that it is readily available for future share purchases? If so, what rate of interest is offered? How does this compare with rates offered elsewhere?

If you intend using a broker's advisory service rather than a 'deals only' service, then ask if you can always deal with the same one or two people in the firm so that they can get to know you better and you can build a better relationship with them. The first time a broker 'takes you on', you may be dealing with a reasonably senior person in the firm: you don't want, after a month or so, to find yourself having to deal instead with a selection of rapidly changing 'juniors' whose knowledge and experience may not be sufficient for your needs. Ask for a few sample copies of the broker's free magazine or investment bulletin. Read it. Does it make sound, sensible reading? If not, choose another broker.

Ask the broker how he deals with the screen-based trading system. Each 'market maker' in each share displays on the trading screens the prices at which he is prepared to deal in each share. For example, it might state that he will buy a particular share at 100p and sell at 105p.

The brokers' 'best execution' rule ensures that deals are done at the best price displayed on the screen. Looking at a share touch price of 100p–105p on the screen, what will the broker do?

If he replies that he will *always* accept the price on the screen, then look for another broker. Why? Because he is lazy.

Sometimes a 'fast market' operates – share prices are dropping like an elephant falling from a skyscraper (or zooming upwards) – when market makers are not held to their screen-quoted prices. This is because as soon as they type in a new price for the shares, so many people sell (or buy) that the screen-prices cannot keep up with what is actually happening. The broker *has* to phone the market maker and make the best deal possible, using the screen-prices as a guide.

Even in normal trading conditions, occasionally a share price spread might be unnecessarily wide. If a share is quoted at 100p to sell and 105p to buy, will the broker be able to haggle on the phone with the market maker and buy shares at 102½p or 104p instead of 105p?

Of course, a lot depends on how many shares you want to buy (or sell) and the size of the company concerned (see also Chapter 10: *What Really Decides A Share Price*). A *good* broker should not be like a battery chicken with his eyes glued to a trading screen accepting absolutely everything that appears before him without question.

If you want to use a cut-price on-line broker, then check if the share prices he displays are the ones you will get if you deal – or are your deals subject to delay and a different price?

Before finalising your choice of broker, check what level of insurance he has to protect you if he gets into difficulties. Some broking firms just rely on the rather limited Investors Compensation Scheme, while others have cover of £1 million or more per client.

There *are* good brokers who can provide an excellent service at a reasonable price – including a computer print-out detailing your investments and their performance since the date you bought them.

When you've found a good broker, treat him properly and you should prosper.

How To Deal With A Broker: 'Understanding'

The art of dealing successfully with a broker is to make sure that he understands what *you* want, and you understand what *he* wants (apart from commissions).

To help in this 'understanding', a broker should send you

a customer agreement letter in which he will set out details of the services his firm can provide. He might well also ask you to complete a form giving him details of your investment objectives and certain other information.

Deal Preparations

Before you contact your broker to make a deal, write on a piece of paper brief details of the deal you intend to do. This helps you remember the basic details.

If you are talking on the phone to your broker, speak clearly. In some cases it is advisable to spell out the name of the shares you are buying/selling as some companies' names sound very similar – particularly on a bad phone line. The difference in share price between two companies with similar-sounding names can be considerable.

Some companies have more than one class of share, with big differences in their price. Are you buying/selling the voting shares or the non-voting shares? Make sure your broker knows *exactly* which shares you wish to buy/sell.

Price Limits

Do you have a price limit at which you want the shares to be bought/sold? For example, do you want the broker to 'deal at best' – the best price he can obtain at the time he does the deal – or is there a price per share at which you would not want your broker to deal at all?

Suppose you have shares in a company that you bought for 150p per share. You look in your morning newspaper and see that those shares are now '195p –5'.

The newspaper indicated by '–5' that the shares had fallen from 200p the day before. Perhaps several large pension funds sold a lot of that company's shares, making the price fall by 10p to 190p and then maybe a large unit trust bought a large number of the shares so the market makers moved the price back to 195p. The market makers by the end of the day might have decided to quote a price of 192½p if you were selling and 197½p if you were buying: the newspaper only gives the *middle* price at which market makers were prepared to deal: 195p is midway between 192½p and 197½p. But that was *yesterday's* price. What will it be today, when you want to sell your shares? Perhaps there will be some bad (or good) news about the company that will make the shares fall further (or rise).

You can therefore tell your broker to 'sell at best' and hope he will get 195p per share, and then find he gets 190p or 200p instead. Or you could tell him to sell the shares at the best possible price, so long as that price is not lower than 188p. If no one wants to buy your shares for 195p, 190p, or even 188p, then you will have to keep them and hope that perhaps a few weeks (or months) later the situation might have changed.

Setting limits is particularly important when buying shares that have been 'tipped' in a newspaper. Suppose the share that was 'tipped' as a good buy was 50p before the 'tip'.

Market makers, on reading the newspaper concerned, will probably think that there will be a good demand for those shares and might quote them at 51p or 52p. Lots of people have read the newspaper. They think the tip is a good one. They rush to buy the shares, forcing the price up to 58p. If you told your broker to deal 'at best', then it may be that *at the time he does your deal* on that day the price is 58p. Shortly after he's done your deal, several large investors in that company decide to take some profits and sell many of their shares. The price falls back to 52p.

The next day you look in the newspaper. Your broker has bought the shares at 58p and yet the newspaper reports the price as being '50p+2'. This is true – the price *was* 50p and at the end of the day the market makers were quoting 50p to sell and 54p to buy, so the middle price was 52p.

It is no good berating your broker for having bought the shares 'at best' for 58p when you could have instructed him to have bought the shares instead for 'not more than 56p each' – in which case the broker would have waited until the price dropped to the level at which you were prepared to buy.

Of course, with some shares the price might not drop to the level at which you are initially prepared to buy them and you therefore either have to raise your 'buying limit' or not acquire the shares at all.

Double-Checking

If you give your instructions to your broker on the phone, ask him kindly to repeat back to you the brief details of your order: this double-checking helps to avoid possible costly mistakes.

The broker may well have tape-recorded your phone conversation – but this is more to safeguard himself against 'mishearings', 'insider dealing accusations', etc. 'Instant playback' is most unlikely to be used unless the broker is very unsure as to the details of the deal you want done. Even then, he is much more likely to phone you back than struggle to find the appropriate part of the tape. With many broking firms, 'instant playback' of taped phone conversations is an impossibility as the recording is done in such a way that the tapes can only be replayed in very special circumstances: otherwise they are locked away.

Contract Notes

After a deal has been done, the broker should send you a contract note which describes the deal: check that the details are correct.

The contract note should state the name of the company in which you have bought (or sold) shares, the number and type of shares bought (or sold), the price per share, the commission and other charges and any other relevant details.

Sometimes when you buy shares you will find the letters **xd** against the share price on the contract note. **xd** means that the shares have been bought *excluding* the benefit of a forthcoming dividend.

Brokers' Advice

If you are using the advisory services of a broker you are not obliged to follow his advice: he may suggest you buy shares which, unknown to him, changing circumstances mean you can't afford; or he might recommend shares in a company whose products you know from bitter experience fall to pieces soon after purchase and so you think (or hope) the company will suffer a severe financial setback.

Don't be afraid of saying 'no' to your broker. He might 'talk posh' (or instead may sound rather 'rough'); he may sound very knowledgeable (and actually *be* very knowledgeable) – but you can still say 'no thanks' to a particular course of action which he might suggest.

The broker is there to serve *you*.

However, you should always be polite when dealing with your broker. That way your broker might pass on some useful investment information about a particular company, or help you get shares in a 'placing' (see also *Placing* on page 59), or perhaps send you a free diary or investment calendar for Christmas!

Record Keeping

Buying and selling shares can give rise to tax liabilities, so you will need to keep a proper record of all your share transactions. Good record keeping can also help you keep track of your investments and assist in deciding whether or not it is time to sell them.

Some people maintain complex records. They have elaborate programs on their home computers and perhaps even draw graphs plotting various share price movements. All this seems rather tedious and time consuming to me. It's all right if you regard playing around with computers as 'fun' and an enjoyable hobby – it's rather a pain if you don't!

Is the time and effort spent on updating share prices every day really worth it for the average private investor? If you really want a computer print-out showing all your investments, their purchase costs, dividend yields, etc. and perhaps even their performance compared with a share index, then your broker can probably provide such valuations every six months or perhaps even quarterly for either a small charge or he may well even provide this service free, depending on the size of your share portfolio.

Each tax year I make two files. Into one I put copies of all the correspondence with my brokers. Into the other I put copies of all the contract notes. I also add details of dividends received. I file the relevant paperwork as soon as it arrives, in order to prevent it getting mislaid.

I also keep records of my share transactions in a note book. I divide each page into a number of columns. In the first column I list the name and number of shares I hold in each company. The next column is the monthly total worth of each shareholding. I can then, at the end of each month, add another column for that month. That way it makes it easier to compare each month's valuation with another.

On a separate sheet of paper I have typed a list of all my shareholdings (which uses both sides of the sheet) with their dates of purchase, the price per share at which each share was bought, and the total purchase cost of each shareholding. I also include details of the months when dividends should be paid. Check for these dates in the companies' reports to shareholders.

When a shareholding is sold I simply cross out its details on the sheet of paper and add the details of any new shares which I might have bought with the sale proceeds.

On the bottom of one side of the sheet of paper are the names, addresses, phone numbers and fax details of my brokers.

This single sheet of paper is invaluable. It enables me instantly to compare my purchase cost per share with the price listed in the daily newspaper, and alerts me to dividend payments which might have been lost in the post.

The sheet accompanies me on foreign business and holiday trips. It would be terrible being in a foreign country and hearing on the radio or TV news that there might be a Stock Market crash and being unable to recall the phone number of your broker and/or the details of your investments: you might then be unable to contact your broker and sell your shares before the crash. It would be like watching someone throw your money down the drain and being frozen to the spot and unable to stop them from doing it. My single sheet of investment information saves me from such problems.

I also keep two other 'record lists' for each tax year. Whenever a dividend cheque arrives I write down the date of the cheque, the name of the company and the amount received.

Whenever I sell a share, I write down the date of the sale, the name of the company concerned, the number of shares sold, the proceeds from the sale, the original cost price and date of purchase of the shares, and the amount of profit or loss made from each deal.

These simple record-keeping systems enable me to keep track of my share transactions, and assist in completing my tax return.

On average, at any one time, I might have shareholdings directly and in my personal pension scheme in about fifty different companies. In total, it only takes me about two hours each month to keep and update these records. Private investors with fewer shareholdings should be able to keep such records in even less time.

However, this system may well not suit everyone, and 'trial and error' will enable you to establish the system that best meets your needs.

What Do They Mean?

Unfortunately, there are a number of words and expressions which it is useful to know in order to understand better what is happening on the Stock Market. What follows are details of some of the most useful words/expressions that have not already been more fully explained earlier in this book (see also Chapter 11: *What Do They Really Mean?*).

AGM: The Annual General Meeting is a meeting which all the voting shareholders of a company are entitled to attend and to vote on the re-election of certain of the directors, the 'adoption' (acceptance) of the annual report and accounts, and on various other matters. If you cannot attend an AGM you can nominate someone to attend and vote on your behalf by completing a proxy form and sending it to the company concerned within the specified time limit.

AIM: The Alternative Investment Market was designed by the London Stock Exchange for 'smaller, young and growing companies'. AIM opened for trading on 19th June 1995.

It is easier for companies to gain admission to AIM than to the main Stock Exchange. Regulatory requirements are fewer, which means that investors should do some careful research *before* investing. As well as checking out all the items mentioned in the next chapter, check the ease of dealing in the shares.

Some companies have such a small number of shares available to the general public, or there is so little interest in the shares, that dealing may be difficult. Check that if you buy the shares you will not be 'locked in' to your shareholding due to lack of investor interest and infrequent dealings.

Shares in AIM companies can be bought via stockbrokers and it can be very helpful to ask their views on a company before buying shares in it.

analyst: An investment *analyst* is a person who analyses the performance of a number of companies and, as a result of that analysis, makes recommendations concerning particular shares, including whether or not they should be bought, held or sold.

bargain: A deal made on the Stock Market is called a *bargain* – even if it is not a 'bargain' in the sense of being a 'good buy'.

bear: Someone who believes that share prices in general will fall in the very near future is a *bear* – the opposite of a bull. Thus, a *bear market* is one in which share prices are falling. Sometimes, a bear will sell shares in the hope of being able to buy them back again at even lower prices.

Big Bang: In the UK, the *Big Bang* was 27th October 1986 when new regulations took effect on the stockbroking system which were mainly intended to increase and encourage competition.

bull: Someone who believes that share prices in general will rise in the very near future is a *bull* – the opposite of a bear. Thus, a *bull market* is one in which share prices are going up and up.

capital gains: The profits made on the sale of shares and other capital assets.

capitalization: The *capitalization* of a company is the total value of all its issued shares, loan stock and other securities at their current market prices. Sometimes, the word *capitalization* is used to describe just the current value of the company's quoted shares.

chartist: Share *chartists* are people who create charts (draw graphs) showing the past price performance of certain shares in the belief that some past patterns of trading will indicate future performance of those shares, thus enabling them to predict whether or not a share should be bought or sold. (As you will see from pages 77-80, I think a lot of the work of chartists is about as meaningful as reading tea leaves.)

dividend: The *dividend* is the amount paid by a company to its shareholders based on the number of shares held and the amount of the company's profits or financial resources which the directors feel should be distributed to shareholders.

Thus, in company reports you will find a statement like: 'The directors recommend a dividend of 1.35p per share' – for each share in that company which you hold you will receive a dividend of 1.35p.

In the US, many companies pay a dividend to their shareholders every quarter. In the UK, companies usually pay dividends twice each year (an *interim dividend* and a *final dividend*) although some companies may only pay one dividend each year and some may not pay any dividend at all – either because they wish to keep all the profits within the company for expansion purposes, or because the company is experiencing 'hard times' and decides it cannot afford to pay dividends to shareholders.

Some companies pay dividends even when they have not earned them. The directors may wish to demonstrate to investors (and potential investors) that they feel the company is in a sound condition and although the company did not earn sufficient in the year concerned to cover the dividend, they believe that the following year the company's earnings will show a significant improvement.

How can a company pay out more in dividends than it has earned in profits? By using some of the cash which the company may have on deposit with a bank from reserves built up over previous, more profitable, years; or some companies occasionally borrow money in order to maintain their track record for paying dividends.

I am always wary of companies that pay out more in dividends than they have earned in the year: they should be closely examined before investing in them. Are the directors' rosy forecasts for future profits likely to be met? If the directors have large shareholdings, are they waiving their dividend entitlements? If not, could their decision to maintain the dividend have been partly influenced by their own wish to receive dividends on their shares?

A company that pays a dividend it has not earned may well have dedicated directors and genuinely excellent future prospects – but it is still best to do some further research before investing in such companies.

dividend cover: The number of times a company could pay its most recent annual amount of dividend from its annual earnings.

For example, suppose a company made after-tax profits of £10 million. It has 250 million shares in issue so, theoretically, it could pay 4p per share dividend and use all £10 million of the profits for this purpose. Instead, the company pays 2p per share dividend. As the company had sufficient profits to pay twice that amount, the dividend cover is 2.

earnings per share: A company's earnings (its net profits after paying taxes, etc.) divided by the number of shares issued produces the company's *earnings per share*.

For example, a company with net profits of £1 million, and 10 million shares, has earnings per share of 10p.

equities: Ordinary shares are also known as *equities*.

flotation: When a company first has its shares offered on the Stock Market this is called a *flotation*.

going public: A private company which announces that it is converting to a public company by floating its shares on the Stock Market is said to be *going public*.

institutional investor: *Institutional investors* are organizations like banks, pension funds, unit trusts, and insurance companies which operate investment funds.

intangible asset: An *intangible asset* is an asset that is not a tangible asset – it is something that is not a 'physical asset'. For example, intangible assets can include copyrights, patent rights and trade marks.

issued shares/shares in issue: Every company has to have an 'authorized share capital' – a given number of shares which it is allowed to create under the terms of its articles (one of the legal documents which first established the company). If a company wishes to increase that number of shares, it has to gain the approval of its shareholders to do so. However, a company may have an authorized share capital of, say, 10 million £1 shares but have only 'issued' (given out or sold) 7 million of them – the remaining 3 million shares remain 'unissued'. Thus, the *issued shares* of a company are those that have been given out or sold to shareholders. Unissued shares have no voting rights until they are issued and thus become issued shares.

liquid assets: Cash or other assets which can easily be sold for cash. If an investor sells most or all of his share portfolio for cash he is said to have *gone liquid*.

liquid market: If a company's shares are traded on the Stock Market easily and regularly, then there is a *liquid market* in the shares: there is a flow of dealings.

However, with some small companies, dealing may be more difficult. Perhaps it may only be possible to buy and sell comparatively small numbers of shares – or maybe very few people wish to deal at all: in which case it may be said that there is an *illiquid market*.

listed company: A *listed company* is a company which has its shares listed (quoted) on a Stock Market.

management buy-out: The purchase of a company by its management, usually with the help of finance provided by one or more institutional investors, is known as a *management buy-out*.

Quite often, the buy-out is of a subsidiary company of a larger, 'parent' company. Sometimes, the parent disposes of the subsidiary company because it wishes to focus on its other activities, or the subsidiary company has performed rather poorly and the parent believes it can make better use of the cash raised from selling the subsidiary company and/or the parent feels that the subsidiary will produce a better performance if 'set free' from the parent.

A cynic might say that amongst the hundreds of management buy-outs there must have been at least one or two where the management of a subsidiary let it turn in poor profits so that the parent was more willing to sell it to them, and at a reasonable price. Having acquired the company, the managers then work as hard as perhaps they ought to have done when the company was part of a large group and transform the company to such an extent that they profit handsomely – especially if the company is eventually sold to another company for a high price or floated on the Stock Market at a price far greater than the managers paid for it in the buy-out.

Of course, some buy-out companies prosper partly because the managers have more control over the company: their decisions are no longer subject to cancellation or change by the head office of a parent company and they no longer have to follow 'head office policy'.

However, if you are a shareholder in a company and you hear that it is selling off one of its subsidiaries to a management buy-out operation, then contact the chairman of the parent company and ask if the buy-out price is the best deal available. Did the parent seek offers from other companies not connected with the management for the subsidiary?

Will the parent company be retaining a shareholding in the buy-out company so that if the former subsidiary performs well, the former parent will also profit from such improved performance?

market maker: In the UK, a *market maker* is a member of a Stock Exchange firm who is obliged to buy and sell shares at all times (and thus 'make a market') in those shares in which he is registered as a principal. This means that a market making firm might, for example, only decide to make a market in the largest 100 quoted companies in Britain, or it might decide to become registered as a market maker in many more companies. For each company in which it acts as market maker it is supposed to guarantee always to quote a price at which it will buy or sell shares.

Many stockbrokers are *not* market makers – instead, they deal for their clients by buying or selling shares via a market-making firm.

It is the market makers who interpret the changing perception of people as to the value of shares by adjusting the prices at which they are prepared to buy or sell shares. Indeed, market makers can (and do) change the prices of shares even if no one is actually buying or selling them!

For example, suppose a market maker hears a rumour that a major institutional investor is about to sell its very large shareholding in a particular company. The market maker may well believe that there will not be sufficient potential buyers of those shares at the current share price, so he 'marks down' the price of those shares in order to tempt buyers.

The institutional investor then denies the rumours that it is to sell the shares concerned and states that it is a 'firm holder' of those shares. The market maker then raises the price at which he is prepared to deal in those shares: yet no shares have actually changed hands – only the price quoted by the market maker has changed.

net asset value: The value of a company after all its debts and other financial obligations have been paid off is its *net* *lue.* This is usually expressed as a net asset value per shai.

For example, suppose a company has 100,000,000 shares. Each share is valued on the Stock Market at £1, so the company's total market capitalization is £100,000,000. The company has land, buildings, stocks of its products and other assets which are worth £150,000,000. However, it also has outstanding bank loans and other debts of £25,000,000. Take away the £25 million of debt from the £150 million of assets and this produces a net asset value of £125 million. Divide the £125 million by the number of shares in issue (100 million) and you end up with a net asset value per share of £1.25p.

The net asset value may, however, be *less* than the current market price of a share, so a share costing £1 might represent a net asset value of only 30p. It depends on the company concerned and the expectations people have for the company's future progress.

OFEX: An unregulated 'off-exchange' trading facility for dealings in shares in unquoted mainly UK registered companies.

penny shares: In the US, a *penny share* is classed as being a share that is priced at less than US$1. In the UK, a penny share used to be regarded as a share quoted at less than about 25p but this 'penny share' definition has gradually been raised so that some people now regard 'penny shares' as being any share priced at less than about 80p. A 'small' share price does not mean that the company concerned is also 'small' – it may have hundreds of millions of shares. Thus, a company with a share price of, say, 50p but with 350 million issued shares has a Stock Market 'worth' of £175 million, while a company with a share price of 375p but with only 10 million issued shares has a Stock Market 'worth' of £37.5 million.

placing: Sometimes new shares in a company are *placed*: instead of being offered to the public at large, the shares are sold to certain institutional and other investors at an agreed price.

price-earnings ratio or **p/e:** A *price-earnings ratio* is a company's current share price divided by its last published earnings per share.

For example, suppose a company has 10 million ordinary shares and the company made a profit after tax of £1 million: the profit attributable to each share is therefore 10p (£1 million of profit divided by 10 million shares). This does *not* mean that the company will pay out 10p per share in dividend. Indeed, it may well only pay a dividend of 1p or 2p per share – the rest of the profit might be retained by the company to help its expansion plans and generally improve its operations. The p/e ratio pays no attention to the amount of dividend – only to the amount of profit.

If the current share price of a company is 200p, then the price-earnings (p/e) ratio, with 10 million shares in issue, and with profits of £1 million, is 20 (200p share price divided by 10p per share profit).

If the £1 million of profit and the 10 million shares in issue remained the same, but the share price was 150p, instead of 200p, then the p/e would be 15.

privatization: *Privatization* is the sale of nationalized or Government-owned industries/activities to the public.

prospectus: The formal document which a company publishes in order to issue new shares and/or be floated on the

Stock Market is called a *prospectus*. The prospectus will include financial and other details about the company in order to try and attract investors to buy shares in the company.

quoted: A *quoted* company is a company that is listed on a stock market.

share portfolio: A person who owns shares in a number of different companies has a *share portfolio* – a collection of shares.

shell company: A *shell company* is a company that has a Stock Market quotation and usually a small capitalization, but has limited activities so that it might possibly be attractive to an entrepreneur wanting a 'vehicle' into which he can 'inject' (put) additional assets and/or steer into greater activities and thus build up the company and also (hopefully) the company's value and share price.

spread: The *spread* is the difference between the market maker's buying price and his selling price.

stop-loss: Some investors place *stop-loss* limits on the shares that they buy: this means that they limit or stop their losses by setting a price at which they will sell certain shares and, if they fall to that level, then they will sell them.

For example, suppose an investor buys shares in a company for 150p each. He may believe that the company is involved in a particular activity which will either make the share price rise steeply or will cause the share price to plummet. He therefore sets a stop-loss limit at, say, 120p. If the shares fall to 120p he will cut his losses and therefore avoid losing even more money should the shares fall still further.

However, suppose the company concerned produces good results and the shares rise from his 150p purchase price to 200p. The investor might then change his stop-loss limit to 175p. If the shares fall to 175p he will sell them, thus ensuring that at least he will keep some of the profits on his share purchase.

It is the investor's responsibility to monitor the market carefully and to activate his stop-loss limits, although a few stockbrokers offer a stop-loss service within certain limits and conditions.

Unfortunately, when there is a sudden, sharp general downturn in the market, it may well not be possible to sell the shares at the stop-loss limit, as the market is falling too rapidly for action to be taken in time. The shares might then have to be sold below the stop-loss price limit. But, in other circumstances, the stop-loss limit can prove very useful.

Stop-loss limits do not necessarily have to be set in stone. I treat them as the 'warning bell' to remind me that when I originally set the stop-loss level I was concerned that if the shares fell to that level there might be something seriously wrong with the company's prospects and the shares could fall further.

I then investigate the reasons for the fall in the share price to my stop-loss level. Is it because the market as a whole has fallen? If so, is it likely that the market will perk up again in the near future?

Have the shares fallen as a result of analysts anticipating bad news in a forthcoming profits statement from the company? What other reasons explain the fall in the share price?

After careful evaluation, I may well sell the shares at, or near, the stop-loss level – or I may decide to re-adjust the stop-loss level downwards slightly because I feel the shares will soon be going up again.

suspensions: Shares can be *suspended* by the Stock Exchange for a variety of reasons. The suspension means that the shares cannot be traded on the Exchange until the suspension has been lifted.

Sometimes, a company's directors and/or brokers ask for the shares to be suspended pending an announcement concerning the company's financial situation, or news of a merger or take-over approach or for some other reason that might create a 'false market in the shares': people trading without knowledge of a particular event that may have a significant effect on the share price.

A share suspension may also be ordered by the Exchange if it is concerned about some action (or inaction) on the part of the directors or for some other reason which it feels could adversely affect shareholders if dealings were to continue in the shares of the company without further details of certain matters being publicly announced.

Sometimes, share suspensions are followed by good news – such as a generous take-over approach for the company. Unfortunately, quite often share suspensions are the prelude to a bad news announcement and sometimes the shares can remain suspended for a lengthy period and/or the company announces that it is in severe financial difficulties. Occasionally, some companies go straight from suspension into receivership with investors losing their entire investment in the company.

tangible asset: An asset that has a physical existence – like cash in the bank, buildings and machinery – is a *tangible* asset.

underwriters: *Underwriters* are investors, bankers and financial institutions which agree (usually for a fee) to purchase any shares offered for sale in a flotation, rights issue, or as part of a bid – the shares they agree to purchase being those which the public or particular shareholders do not want. The underwriters may then keep the shares purchased, for their own benefit or, very often, will eventually dispose of them to other investors.

yield: The _yield_ is the percentage rate of return on an investment.

Chapter 3:

What To Look For In A Share

When my daughter, Kimberley, was three years old she came to me just before Christmas, clutching a 20p coin. She must have heard me talking about penny shares as she said: 'Daddy, I've got some money here for you. You can buy your own shares for Christmas with it. But you can only buy shares that will go up.'

I carefully explained that I could not guarantee that the shares would go up. 'Oh,' said Kimberley, 'then buy yourself a packet of crisps with the money instead.'

No one is infallible. There are few 'sure things' in the investment world. So what follows is based on some of my own personal experiences – and sometimes I would have been better off buying packets of crisps instead!

Share Attractions

There are a number of features about particular shares that will attract my investment attention, such as:

Take-Overs

They seem likely take-over targets (see Chapter 6: *How To Find Take-Over Targets*).

Director Dealings

One or more of the directors of a company have recently announced that they have bought more shares in it. If they have faith in the shares, surely the company must be performing well?

For example, I once read a very small item in the *Financial Times* which revealed that the chairman of a particular company had increased his shareholding in it, so that he now owned 17.5 per cent of the company. I felt that if he had such faith in his company, then perhaps it was worth an investment.

I decided to find out some more details of the company. It had property, engineering, motor distribution and other interests, and appeared to be doing well. I therefore bought some shares in it for 75p each.

The company continued to perform well and less than one year later I was able to sell the shares for 297p each.

Not all announcements of purchases of shares by directors lead to increases in the share price: sometimes, the price actually goes *down* – especially if it is believed that directors are increasing their shareholdings in order to thwart a take-over bid.

It has also been known for some directors to buy shares in order to help support the share price. They have borrowed heavily against their original shareholding in the company and if the share price falls too far, then the lender may ask them for additional security which they might find difficult to provide. So they borrow to buy more shares in the company, pledging those shares as security for the new loan. They hope that the announcement of their buying activity will attract others to buy shares in the company and so the share price will either rise or at least be maintained at what, for the directors concerned, is a more comfortable level.

Therefore, do *not* get carried away with enthusiasm for a company just because it has been announced that a director has bought more shares in it. *Check it out.* Does the company have solid assets and good prospects?

Price-earnings ratios

The shares have a relatively low p/e ratio compared to other companies in the same sector. Is the low p/e due to the company having been 'overlooked' by institutional buyers, or is the p/e simply reflecting fears of a possible downturn in profits? If the former, perhaps the shares might be worth investigating further.

For example, I was once struck by the comparatively low p/e of a small publishing firm compared with some other publishers. I obtained a copy of the company's annual report and saw that it had a reasonable track record for profits, it appeared to be well managed, and its books were attractive.

I therefore bought some shares, paying 290p each. Within two years I sold some of them for 585p each.

It is important to compare p/e ratios with companies within the same sector (as well as with the market as a whole) because p/e ratios can vary greatly between different sectors of the market.

Assets

A company has assets worth considerably more per share than its share price. The weekly magazine, *The Investors Chronicle*, is an invaluable source of information on asset values of British companies, as its analyses of company results frequently give details of the net asset value per share of the companies reviewed. (See also Chapter 4: *What To Look For In A Company Report.*)

Dividends

The shares provide a good dividend income, superior to that of many other companies, *and* the prospects of the company concerned appear to be very good.

Shareholder Perks

My wife sometimes makes a small investment in a company simply to make use of the 'perks' which some companies give to their shareholders. These perks can include significant discounts on hotel accommodation, cars, clothes, jewellery, etc.

However, there is little point in buying shares in a company that has an over-inflated share price just to gain a discount worth perhaps £50, if the company's share price might suddenly collapse and cost you considerably more than that £50 'saving'. Your stockbroker should be able to advise you on such matters.

Small Companies

I am particularly attracted to small companies. One of the reasons for this is that some of them are likely to grow at a far faster rate than many of the much larger companies.

It is much more likely that a small company might be able to increase its profits from, say, £1 million to £1.5 million in one year, than it would be for a much larger company to turn profits of £500 million into £750 million within the same short period.

If the small companies are also classed as having 'penny

shares' (the shares cost less than about 80p each), then this can increase their attractions for purely speculative dealing.

It is important to remember that a 'penny share' does *not* necessarily indicate that a company is small: it may have many hundreds of millions of shares in issue.

However, if the company concerned has a low capitalization *and* its shares are less than 80p each, *and* the company appears to have good prospects – then its shares might be worth considering as a possible investment.

Suppose an investor has £5,000 to invest. There are two equally attractive companies, A and B. Both are well managed, produce good profits, and appear to have an attractive future. The companies are capitalized at, say £10 million each – but one company (A) has 4 million issued shares, with the share price being 250p; and the other company (B) has 40 million issued shares, with the current quoted share price being 25p.

Thus, each company has the same value, but for his £5,000, an investor can buy only 2,000 shares in company A, whereas he could, instead, purchase 20,000 shares in company B. Psychologically, being able to get more shares for the same money appeals to some investors. If many of them buy shares in company B as a result of this, then the shares will go up.

Changes in the market, company results, etc., are also likely to affect the share prices of A and B – but a share price rise of 2.5p means only a profit of £50 for an investor with 2,000 shares which he bought for 250p per share; while a 2.5p per share increase means a profit of £500 to the investor with 20,000 shares which he bought for 25p each. Theoretically, of course, if both companies produced equally good results, their share price should rise as a *percentage* of their former price, not by 2.5p or the same amount in pence terms for each company. But theory doesn't always work, and the lower-priced share benefits!

It is important to make quite sure before you invest in a

company, thinking it is 'small', that it really is as small as you think it is. For example, you may look at a company's market capitalization as listed in a newspaper and see that this is given as being, say, £18 million, based on the current price of its ordinary shares which might, perhaps, be in 'penny share territory'.

But if you double-check with the company's annual report you may find that, in addition to ordinary shares, the company has also issued, say, over £35 million of convertible preference shares of £1 each.

The company may still be worth an investment, but it is not as 'small' as you once thought it was. Also, check on what basis the convertible preference shares have been issued – on what formula can they be converted into ordinary shares?

If, say, the current share price is only around 30p and the convertible preference shares have conversion rights at well over £2 per ordinary share, then what is the reason for this wide disparity in price?

Were the convertible preference shares issued many years ago when the company was performing so well that its ordinary shares were much higher than they are today and it then appeared 'realistic' that the ordinary shares might rise well above the conversion price? If so, then what happened subsequently to make the ordinary shares fall to current penny share levels – considerably below the conversion right price? Does the company still have the same management as it did at the time of the convertible preference share issue – or has it been replaced or reinvigorated? Does the company really have an excellent chance of improving its profits and prospects?

Not all penny shares are 'good buys' – some should be positively avoided because they are unlikely to produce good results. You have to be very choosy in your share selections, and sometimes a large company will prove to be a much better investment than a small company.

Turn-Round Potential

A company with 'turn-round' potential can sometimes be a good investment. Perhaps a company has fallen on hard times, shown a sharp reduction in profits (or maybe even produced a loss) and the shares have fallen heavily.

If the management has shown that it is taking strong action to remedy the situation by, perhaps, selling off some assets, streamlining its operations, improving its products and sales teams, etc., then possibly the shares might be worth a speculative purchase.

Management Changes

A formerly rather 'sleepy' company has announced that its management team has been changed, or considerably strengthened, by the arrival of a new managing director or chief executive who has an excellent track record with other companies. Maybe he will 'spark some life' into the company (particularly if he is being rewarded by share options or bonuses paid on results) and so this formerly unattractive company might now possibly prove to be an excellent investment.

Personal Experience Pays: Work

Personal experience can show you share bargains – and can also show you some of the shares to avoid.

What do you do for a living? Has the company you work for recently changed one of its major suppliers? If so, perhaps you should investigate the investment potential of that new supplier: maybe its products are better and cheaper than its rivals, or its service much superior – in which case, perhaps it might prove to be a rapidly expanding and profitable company. Check it out.

Is your company involved in a major re-equipping exercise? If so, then do the producers of the new machines look as if they might be about to cash in on a boom in re-equipping by many other companies, too?

Is your own company performing extremely well? If so, and it is a quoted company, then why not invest in it? But make sure you comply with any 'insider trading' legislation: your company secretary and/or stockbroker should be able to advise you on this.

Is your company re-locating to another part of the country and selling its 'old' office block or factory premises for an extremely high price? If so, then look at your 'old' neighbouring companies; perhaps they have considerably undervalued the worth of their buildings and land in their accounts and, if they moved too, they could realize the true value of those assets.

Reading

Local knowledge can sometimes be useful for pointing towards shares to be bought – or sold. Local newspapers have often been the first with the news of firms 'in trouble': perhaps a local factory has just made many of its employees redundant or has closed down completely. They can also lead on 'success stories': local companies applying for planning permission to expand their premises; and successful local entrepreneurs who are aiming for Stock Market flotations for their firms.

Use the information in a local newspaper to do your own further research. For example, if a factory has closed down, go and look at the factory site. Is there a notice stating that it has been acquired by developers – perhaps for a new superstore or warehouse complex or for some other purpose? If so, then further research may lead to a company whose shares might benefit from this new development: perhaps the developer, if it acquired the site very cheaply.

If the local newspaper gives details of the opening of a new corporate headquarters building, then go and look at it. If the building looks luxurious, then it could be a *bad* sign: maybe the directors are more interested in status than in running a lean, efficient (and highly profitable) company?

Do you have some time on your hands? If so, then a visit to a major public library might prove rewarding. Glance through copies of some of the latest specialist magazines: ones about advertising, agriculture, banking, building, etc. Maybe you will see an item about an advertising agency that is expected to win a major new account that might greatly increase its profits: do the shares in that agency fully reflect that potential in their price?

Has a particular company announced the appointment of a PR firm/merchant banker well known for its expertise in defending companies against take-over bids? If so, then perhaps the company is worried it may soon come under 'attack' from a bidder? Are the shares likely to rise steeply if a bid actually happened?

Look at details of staff changes. Perhaps a highly respected contracts manager of a major building firm has left to join a much smaller company: is it possible that he might have changed jobs in order to help build up that company and its profits (and share price)?

Shopping

Look around the shops. Do there seem to be far more sales than at the same time last year? Could this indicate that spending by customers is generally falling and so frequent 'sales' have to be announced in order to entice them into the shops? If so, then perhaps store company shares should be regarded with a bit more caution than before.

Perhaps you have noticed a brand new shop that has recently opened and appears always to be full of enthusiastic customers? If so, then the shares in the company that owns that shop might possibly be worthy of further consideration.

Have you bought a new gadget that you think is excellent and has few (or no) rivals? If so, who makes it? Maybe the details of the company concerned should be looked at to see if its shares might present a good investment opportunity.

Have you bought a car, CD player or some other item and it has broken down soon after purchase and the attitude of the service personnel is to shrug their shoulders and generally show that they couldn't care less about the problem? If so, and some of your friends and colleagues have had similar problems with the same product – then perhaps the shares in the manufacturer/retailer concerned should be avoided, as sooner or later, if their products/service do not improve, they will eventually lose so much business to better competitors that they should experience a drop in profits and consequently a fall in their share price.

What do your children, friends, relatives, and work colleagues spend their money on? Can their favourite products/shops/activities point the way to possible investment opportunities?

Travel

When travelling abroad, look around you: trends in one country may later be followed in another. For example, some years ago I noticed that competition amongst US consumer electronics retailers was intense. According to the *Miami Herald*, there were, 'Too many stores, too few sales and too many products in the market place,' which led to, 'lower prices and lower profit margins'.

I was therefore concerned at that time that such competition would be repeated in the UK and so, despite various 'share tipsters' proclaiming the merits of a particular UK consumer electronics retailer, I avoided the shares. This prevented me from suffering financially when the shares more than halved in less than a year.

Shares To Avoid

It is important to remember that successful investing is not only investing in shares that go *up*, but *not* investing in shares that are likely to go *down*. Personal experience can prevent an investment that might perform poorly but which, at first sight, perhaps seemed almost attractive.

For example, I once noticed that the share price of a small grocery stores group appeared to be rather depressed compared with the rest of the groceries/stores sector. Perhaps it was an overlooked bargain? Maybe it had turn-round potential?

Then I discovered that the group were opening a new store in the area where I lived. I decided to wait and see how the new store performed before I bought any of the company's shares.

When the shop eventually opened it appeared to be clean, smart, and had long opening hours. Unfortunately, although it had no direct competition in the immediate neighbourhood, its prices for many of the goods which it sold were so high that many people preferred to shop for their groceries and other items elsewhere. The product range was also not exactly suitable for the locality concerned. The store also tried to sell a large quantity of fresh food – but failed to attract sufficient custom. I envisaged severe dents to profits when such unsold food had to be disposed of since, unlike tinned and frozen produce, there was insufficient sales time available to send much of it to another store in a different part of the country before the food went bad.

I therefore did *not* invest in the company's shares. Within a year, the shares were languishing at less than half the price from when I first looked at them, and they subsequently fell still further. The shop which I had observed opening closed within two years.

Share Tipsters

Some share tipsters are very good – others are terrible. Try to assess their track records before investing in any of their 'tipped' shares and, if possible, try to check out whether or not the 'tipped' company is likely to perform to the extent which the 'tipster' has claimed.

One of the problems with 'tips' that appear in newspapers and on websites is that thousands (if not millions) of people will probably read of the same 'tip' at the same time. Some of the readers may rush in and buy the shares, forcing them to rise to a ludicrous height from which they might soon fall as earlier investors take advantage of the sudden steep share price increase to sell all or part of their shareholding and take some good profits.

A patient investor might find it better to wait for a 'corrective fall' (which brings the share price back to a more realistic level) before he buys the shares, rather than rushing in with the herd on the day the 'tip' first appeared. Of course, a corrective fall does not always happen, and the shares might remain highly priced.

Tips from friends can be deadly. I once bought shares in a small UK company for 44.5p each. Soon after purchase, the share price plunged and, within a few weeks, I cut my losses at 27p per share. Fortunately, I had invested only a modest amount. If I had not cut my losses when I did, I would have suffered even more as the company's shares plunged much further.

Why had I bought the company's shares? I knew nothing about the company at the time – I was relying on a friend's 'hot tip': he had read something somewhere that the company's share price would soon rocket. I thought it might be worth a small, speculative punt . . .

This experience reinforced my previously strongly held resolution (broken when I bought the shares on my friend's 'tip') that I would never buy a share without first researching the company concerned.

The delay in double-checking information in a 'tip' has meant that I have missed out on a few 'ground floor' purchases – but it has also saved me from making a number of investments that would have proved disastrous.

Would you buy a new car without test-driving it, or at least finding out about its mechanical capabilities? Would you buy some new clothes without feeling the quality of the material or seeing if they were the right size? Almost certainly not – so why do so many people use their hard-earned money to buy shares in companies about which they know nothing?

It nearly always pays to know something about a company *before* you invest in it.

Even when many 'tipsters' and 'experts' are recommending people to buy shares in a particular company – or in companies in a certain sector of the market – remember that there might be a possibility that they are all wrong.

An interesting visit can be made to a reference library to look at newspapers and magazines from July and August 1987: how many 'experts' were still saying the market would continue to go *up*? Did *you* believe them at that time?

Indeed, how many highly paid investment advisers, fund managers, stockbrokers, analysts and tipsters were saying that there was 'nothing to worry about' and that there would *not* be a sharp downturn in the market?

The same was true in 1929: many 'experts' and tipsters failed to warn of the Crash in time – simply because they did not realize that it could happen in the way it did.

Even when 'tipsters' are recommending the sale of a particular share – or even claiming the imminent arrival of a general market downturn – consider the possibility that they might be mistaken. If lots of people follow their advice and share prices fall, might this then create buying opportunities? Sometimes, if you can take a long-term view, the best time to buy something is when no one else wants it, so you can acquire it at a bargain price.

By all means read the advice of tipsters – but don't necessarily follow the herd. Do what *you* feel is right: at least if you get it wrong it's your *own* decisions and experience you'll be learning from!

Chartists And Gurus

'It's in the charts – the shares will rise.' Sometimes, such a claim is about as accurate as trying to predict the future from tea leaves, or from studying the entrails of a goat.

Just because something has happened once before (or even a number of times) does not necessarily mean that a pattern has developed that will continue in the future, even if it does produce a nice-looking chart.

If chartists are all so clever, then how is it that many of the firms for which they work lost lots of money in the Crash of '87?

If a chart of an individual company's performance could nearly always accurately predict its future share price performance, then why are so many chartists still not millionaires from their own personal investment successes?

This is not to say that charts (and chartists) are completely useless. Charts are useful for demonstrating certain trends and for pointing out consequences which might follow if those trends continue. For example, a chart demonstrating that when p/e ratios in the UK and US reach a particular height, a downturn in the market has, in the past, almost invariably taken place, will alert investors to watch out for the p/e warning signals.

A chart can also reveal patterns of share-buying: perhaps investors are prepared to buy a particular company's shares up to a certain level but, when the shares reach a certain price, other investors are possibly attracted into selling their shares in the company. This might indicate the 'bottom' and the 'top' level for the share price in the short to medium-term.

However, charts are of little use in predicting that the founding shareholders of a company have quarrelled, and one of them proposes to sell his sizeable shareholding. Or, perhaps the company's main products have come under severe competition from higher quality, lower-priced products, or they may soon even become obsolete. Nor can charts accurately predict the actions of managers with their hands in the till, political assassinations, etc. – all of which can have a serious effect on the share price of a company.

Charts cannot predict that a company's chairman is going to be killed in a car crash and be replaced by a dynamic person who changes the entire management team so that the company transforms itself from a plodding, 'going nowhere' company into one of the stars of the Stock Market.

Charts cannot predict that a company's research laboratory will suddenly produce a cure for a particular illness that will transform the company's fortunes.

Suppose there were chartists in the days of the quill pen – would they have accurately predicted the coming of the typewriter and its effect on various pen manufacturers?

Did chartists predict the invention of television or personal computers or fax machines? Chartists cannot predict invention: and I doubt if they can accurately predict very many of the *consequences* of many inventions.

In real life, there are far too many uncertainties and imponderables for everything to be neatly set out on a chart with the future always being accurately mapped out.

Thus, so long as you only regard charts as an *indicator* of a *possible trend* or event, and do not rely on them totally to choose your investments, then they can sometimes be of some assistance.

As for investment gurus: some of them are right about as many times as a stopped watch, but people only remember the gurus' successes and forget all the many times that the gurus were wrong.

Some gurus qualify everything and/or write in a style that makes it possible for their words to be interpreted (after the event) in almost any way they want.

To hear some gurus talk on TV and radio, you could be forgiven for thinking that they are frequently wrong, but never in doubt.

Again, not all investment gurus speak and write rubbish. A number of them make their pronouncements only after a great deal of research, or have so absorbed the spirit of the share marketplace that even their 'hunches' and 'feelings' may quite often be proved right.

Therefore, listen to what some of the gurus have to say – but use them only as an indicator as to possible shares which might be worth further investigation.

With both chartists and gurus, there can be an element of 'self-fulfilling prophecy'. Suppose sufficient people believe a chartist or guru when he says 'shares in company A will do well' or 'the market is heading for a dramatic crash' and they all rush out and buy shares in company A – or sell all their shares hoping to beat a crash.

The consequences of their actions will be that company A's shares will have gone up or (with so many people selling all their shares) the market generally will have gone down.

The chartist or guru can then say: 'I told you so.' But if he had kept quiet, would company A's shares have risen or the market generally gone down? (See also Chapter 10: *What Really Decides a Share Price?*)

A Bit Of Everything?

In my investment portfolio, I now always try to include some shares in a number of small companies which I hope will eventually grow into large companies; some shares in 'speculative situations' (companies – large or small – with take-over or turn-round possibilities, etc); and some shares in companies that provide a reasonable dividend income.

Such a portfolio may well not suit everyone. When I first started investing I had to choose mainly speculative shares because that was the only way I could quickly make enough money to allow a wider spread of investments.

Some people may not want to 'gamble' on speculative ventures and may prefer, instead, to opt for more staid companies in which to invest. Other people may only want to buy shares in companies that are potential takeover targets, turn-round situations, possible discoverers of platinum or gold mines, or possible inventors of new drugs or other potentially highly successful products.

For whatever reason you invest, you don't want to make an overall loss on your share portfolio, so choose your shares carefully. By all means take a gamble (if you can afford to lose) – and remember that some gambles are more sensible than others.

Your investment strategies and the types of shares you choose should match your own character and the needs of yourself and family (if any). It is too easy to make mistakes in investing if you try too hard to act out of character.

A person should not, for example, gamble on lots of speculative 'penny shares' if, by nature, he is not a great risk taker: he might well pick some 'wrong' shares and perhaps panic when they perform badly. A more 'balanced' portfolio would perhaps be better for such a person.

Timing Matters: Company Announcements

Some people buy shares just ahead of the announcement of a company's results, in the hope that if the results are good, the share price will rise.

Unfortunately, brokers' analysts will usually have circulated some months in advance of the results their estimates of the company's likely profits and so the share price might already have gone up in the expectation of good results. Then, if the analysts' estimates prove to be wrong, and the company concerned announces disappointing results that are well below expectations, the shares will probably fall.

However, if you think the analysts might have underestimated the profits to be announced by a particular company, then you might still make some money.

Most analysts tend to follow the larger companies. Perhaps you can find one of the smaller companies which analysts have overlooked and try to work out whether or not its profits will show a significant improvement on last year's figures. Has the company carved a profitable niche in a rapidly expanding area of activity? Has it recently sold any property or other assets at a large profit? Has the share price hardly moved for months? Is it underrated by the market?

Ask your broker to give (or sell) you an investment calendar. This should include the dates of many likely company announcements regarding annual and interim results. It might also include some of the dates when it is expected that there will be various official announcements regarding UK economic statistics such as the UK Official Reserves figures, Public Sector Borrowing figures, Provisional Retail Sales figures, and so on. Also look out for forthcoming announcement dates of such figures in newspapers and on financial websites.

How can you use this information? Suppose you are thinking about buying shares in a small or medium sized property company, and you notice that in a few weeks' time a number of major property companies are due to announce their annual results. If you feel that those results will be poor, then you might consider delaying the purchase of the shares in the small/medium property company until *after* the announcement of the major company's results, as it could be that their poor figures will result in not only their own shares being marked down, but those of many other property companies too.

Similarly, announcements by major companies in other sectors can also sometimes influence the share prices of companies sharing the same sector.

Trade Figures

If an announcement is due of, say, UK Retail Sales figures, and you think the figures will show a downturn in trade, then consider delaying any purchase of shares in the stores sector until *after* the announcement of the figures, as 'bad' sales news might well depress the whole of the retail stores sector.

Other economic statistics are dealt with in Chapter 10: *What Really Decides a Share Price?*

Index Changes

The FT-SE 100 Index is based on the performance of the largest (based on their market value) 100 UK registered companies listed on the UK Stock Exchange.

Sometimes, a company is taken over and so it is removed from the Index and replaced by another company.

Sometimes, a fast-growing company becomes large enough to displace one of the companies in the FT-SE 100 Index, or perhaps a company suffers a severe setback in its share price, thus reducing its market value, and its reduced worth makes it no longer eligible for inclusion in the Index.

Keep an eye on company capitalizations (listed on the share price pages of the *Financial Times* and a number of other newspapers). If you see that a company is soon likely to be included in the Index, then you could consider buying its shares *before* its inclusion, in the hope that the institutional investors operating 'index-tracking' funds will have to buy shares in that company in order to continue to 'track' the FT-SE 100 Index. This weight of institutional buying could help make the share price of the company concerned to rise.

Similarly, if it looks likely that a company will be 'dropped' from the FT-SE 100 Index, then it might be advisable to wait until some time *after* the company has actually been 'dropped' before buying its shares. This is because some of the index-tracking funds will have to dispose of their shareholdings in that company (as it is no longer in the Index) and this institutional selling can depress the share price of the company concerned. However, the 'compilers' of the FT-SE 100 do not 'drop' a company immediately its capitalization falls below being the 100th largest: to bring some stability to the Index they monitor the performance of other companies too, and will only 'drop' a company if it has fallen to about 110th in capitalization ranking. Companies included in some other indices can be monitored in a somewhat similar way.

Time Differences

International time differences are also used by a number of investors to make profits (and losses). For example, suppose Wall Street has fallen sharply, perhaps due to reaction to some official announcement of US trade or other economic figures. That market closes *after* the London market has closed. Therefore, when the London market opens the next day, the chances are that market makers will initially quote lower prices for a number of UK shares – particularly those with large US interests. The market makers are concerned that the London market might follow Wall Street downwards, perhaps feeling that 'Wall Street's sneezes will spread diseases'.

If an investor believes that Wall Street will 'perk up again', then he can buy UK shares early in the morning that have been marked down due to the Wall Street fall the previous day. He can then hope that when Wall Street recovers, the UK Stock Market will 'pick up again' too. Indeed, the investor might hope that by around 3.25pm in the UK, when Wall Street has only been open a short time, shares in the UK will be marked up again if Wall Street has started its day with a sharp rise. The investor could then sell the shares he had bought that morning.

Quick deals like this are very risky, and the profits per share are likely to amount to perhaps, at most, only a few pence, so an investor would need to deal in fairly large numbers of shares if minimum commission charges are not going to 'eat away' all his profits.

Options Links

Some investors are interested in the links between options trading and the prices of shares.

For example, they might look in the *Financial Times* and see that there is a lot of business being done in 'call' options. A 'call' option gives an investor/speculator the right to purchase shares in a particular company at a certain, fixed price within a specified time period.

If lots of 'call' business is being done in a particular company's shares, then it can indicate that some investors/ speculators believe that the price of the shares will go up. They hope to be able to exercise their 'call' options and, by doing so, hopefully buy the shares at less than their market price on a particular day so that they can then sell those shares at a profit.

An investor noticing lots of 'call' option business in a particular company's shares might then (if there is not also a lot of 'put' option business – the right to sell the shares) buy some of the company's shares, hoping that they will go up. Thus an investor can use such option activity as a pointer towards certain shares which might be worth further investigation as to their investment merits.

When To Sell

Almost as important as buying the right shares is knowing when to sell them.

There is a tremendous temptation amongst investors to hold on to badly performing shares in the hope that they will 'come right': they don't want to admit they've made a mistake in buying them.

'I know the profits are down, the management is useless, the products are dreadful,' some investors tell themselves, 'but this just demonstrates that the company can be regarded as a possible take-over target' – although the investor perhaps originally bought the shares for their then high dividend yield, rather than on any thoughts of take-over potential.

The investor now finds the share price has collapsed, the company is on the verge of (or already making) losses, and the dividend has been cut or abandoned. So why not cut losses before the company perhaps goes into liquidation – or at least suffers some years of depression – before maybe, it is revitalized?

If you were walking up a hill and dropped a bag of groceries and some of them rolled into the road and were flattened by passing vehicles, would you abandon the remaining groceries that were lying on the pavement? And say: 'Oh dear, people might think I'm a bit of a clumsy fool dropping the groceries. If I leave them on the ground and walk away I can pretend that they don't belong to me.'

You would almost certainly pick up the 'rescuable' groceries. So why do so many investors 'abandon' even quite large sums of money when they have invested in poorly performing shares, just to avoid admitting to themselves that they made an honest mistake, rather than rescuing as much of their money as possible?

Don't be afraid of admitting a mistake. If you think your shares will fall, sell them.

Loyalty

Now we come to the question of 'loyalty'. You have held some shares for a number of years. The investment has performed well: the dividend income has been good, and the share price has risen nicely.

However, you feel the company is about to hit 'hard times'. What do you do? Stay with the company and keep your investment in it, knowing that the share price will probably fall?

What you do is what you feel: how has the company treated you as a private investor? Has the management responded quickly to any suggestions or queries you might have sent to them? Does the annual report demonstrate that the management *cares* about the shareholders? (See Chapter 4: *What To Look For In A Company Report.*)

Will the 'hard times' be merely a hiccup in the firm's progress, and within a very short time might the company bounce back to even greater profits with a much increased share price?

If the answers to all these questions are rather negative, then sell your shares. Even if the answers are positive, ask yourself if the management are likely to take salary cuts in the event of the 'hard times'; if not, then why should *you* suffer by seeing the value of your investment fall while *they* still get their full salary?

Loyalty to a company has to be *earned.* Many managements never earn it. Some just whine about 'short termism' on the part of investors when it is their own actions and attitudes that have possibly led to it.

But maybe you pay no attention to 'loyalty' anyway and just want to make as much money as possible: if so, sell your shares at the first hint of trouble. Do whatever you feel is right for you.

Greed Risks

Don't be greedy. Some investors know a share is greatly over-priced, yet still they are reluctant to take a very good profit because they feel the shares may go a few pence higher before the price is 'rumbled', and so they hang on, hoping to be able to get out at the very top.

I think the little bit of extra profit is not worth the risk. If the shares are over-priced, they might suddenly collapse, perhaps without any warning and, instead of banking good profits, they are facing losses.

It is very difficult to judge _exactly_ when a share price has reached its peak. So why not take the profits and invest them in something that might turn out to be even more profitable?

In highly speculative shares, I now nearly always sell half my shareholding when the share price has doubled: that way, the remaining shareholding (disregarding tax considerations) has cost me nothing, and so I can take a more generous view of the company's future performance and consider it as a longer-term investment.

In the past, when I had no children, I did not think that way: I was more concerned with getting as much speculative profit as possible so that I could have more funds available for investment. A risk meant relatively little to me then: if a 'gamble' went wrong and I went back to being very poor again and I had to struggle to earn and save another sum for investing, then so what? Having a family now (to me) makes a difference.

Now, not only do I think about making _more_ money from an investment, I also think about _conserving_ and _protecting_ my assets: I don't like the thought of losing too much money. By 'selling on a double', at least if the remaining part of the shareholding performs less well, then I won't have 'lost' my original investment.

Sometimes, if I think one of my investments is unlikely to double, but has still experienced a good rise in value, then I will probably take some profits so that they can be used for other ventures.

'Hanging On'

It is strange (but often true) that many of the people who hang on to poorly performing shares for far too long (rather than cutting their losses before the shares fall even further) are the same people who take profits too soon on their successful share purchases.

If you have an investment in a company that is performing very well, the management is excellent, and the future looks bright, then why sell the shares for a modest profit if the shares are not really speculative, and are likely to go much higher? Unless you need the cash for other (and better) purposes, then why not keep the shares and reap a fuller reward some time later for your investment?

I am sure some people sell shares 'too early' just to be able to prove to themselves that they can make a profit from at least one of their investments, even if it might not make up for the loss they are showing on the poor investments they are reluctant to get rid of.

Sell!

If you have shares in companies where the share price performance has been rather dull, and looks as if it might continue to be dull, then consider selling the shares. Perhaps if you released your funds from the investment you might be able to find another company in which to invest where the performance will hopefully be better.

Finally, even if you've been investing for many years, no one says you *must* continue to invest. If you think the market is going to crash, then sell!

Chapter 4:

What To Look For In A Company Report

First Reactions

What is your immediate reaction to a company report when it first arrives? Does it have a glossy colour photo on the cover, or is it rather plain and dull?

Does it really matter what the cover looks like – surely it's the figures inside that count?

A rather plain cover can indicate either that a company uses its funds carefully and has better things to spend money on (like expansion and improvements to the business) or it might indicate a rather staid and 'traditional' board of directors.

A glossy cover can either show that a company is trying to attract the attention of would-be investors, analysts, financial journalists, etc., as well as trying to give existing shareholders the impression that the company is doing (or hoping to do) well; or it can be used in an attempt to 'hype up' a rather dull, boring and rather 'plodding' company.

However, it really is what's between the covers that matters.

If you are a shareholder in a company and have not already received the annual report, or if you are merely contemplating a possible investment in a firm and would

like to read that document, then write to the Company
Secretary of the company concerned requesting the report,
or see if the company has a website displaying its details.

You can also get information from the *Financial Times*
share price pages on how to obtain reports from many
companies, simply by making one phone or fax call or
making contact via its website.

Some companies issue summary financial statements –
but these omit many of the items in a full report. Make sure
you get the full document.

Most company reports – if you look beyond the photos –
are rather dull and boring, and most people haven't the
time (or patience) to read every word of them – so what are
some of the key points to look out for, besides noting if the
dividend is to be increased from the previous year's level?

Chairman's/Chief Executive's Statement

Look at the last few paragraphs of the Chairman's/Chief
Executive's Statement. This is usually where he states his
hopes and expectations for the immediate future of the
company (see also Chapter 11: *What Do They Really Mean?*).

Is he giving a warning about a possible downturn in
profits? Is he very confident about the future?

Now go back to how he started his statement. Does his
opening paragraph impress you?

Look at the report from the point of view of one of the
owners of the company. The directors have to justify their
actions and performance to *you*. Do they do this successfully, putting over the fact that they have managed the
company well to the benefit of the shareholders and
employees – or is the Chairman's/Chief Executive's statement full of excuses, blaming everyone but himself for the
company's poor performance?

Quickly skim through the rest of the statement. Are there any 'warnings' about huge rises in the costs of raw materials, 'dumping' of low-cost rival products from foreign competitors, new legislation or anything else that might affect the company's sales and profits and which might indicate that perhaps you should sell your shares?

Financial Highlights

Look at any 'financial highlights' – brief summaries of the company's results.

How does the level of turnover compare with the previous year's figure? If it has significantly increased, then have the profits increased, too – or does it look as if the company's profit margins are under pressure?

Auditor's Report

Look out for statements in the Auditor's Report that the Auditors 'have been unable to satisfy themselves' about some aspect of the company's assets, stocks, provision against possible losses or the results of litigation. This could be a warning signal.

What you want to see from the Auditor's Report is that the company has been given a 'clean bill of health' with their assertion that the company's accounts give a true and fair view of the state of affairs of the company.

However, it has been known for auditors to have been misled, mistaken and (rarely) incompetent, and a company has subsequently gone into liquidation as the accounts had *not* given a true picture of the state of the company, even though the auditors had earlier given it a 'clean bill of health'! So still keep an eye out for any adverse press comment on the state of the company.

Notes To The Accounts

It may seem strange to glance at the Notes to the Accounts *before* actually looking at all the figures – but it is in the Notes that significant items can be almost 'hidden'.

Has the method of calculating the depreciation charge been changed from the previous year? For example, if certain items used to be 'written off' over five years, has this now been changed to three years (meaning they have to be replaced much quicker than before) or to seven years (perhaps implying that the company is cutting capital expenditure costs by trying to extend the life of certain items of equipment, etc.)?

Look at the details of the company's borrowings. Is it heavily in debt? Are lots of its borrowings in foreign currencies and, if so, are there likely to be any exchange rate changes that could have a serious effect?

Are there any 'contingent liabilities' for legal actions?

Has the method of funding the pension scheme been changed? Perhaps the company has had to make extra payments into the scheme because it was under-funded in the past; or perhaps it has reduced its pension fund payments because the fund has performed extremely well or staff numbers have fallen. If the company's contributions to the fund have changed, then what effect has this had on the company's profits? Is this likely to be a 'one-off' effect, or will it continue for a number of years?

Have there been any changes in the valuation of stocks? I am always cautious about stock valuations – particularly of 'creative products': films, books, video cassettes, TV rights, etc.

A film (or the rights to a TV series) may have cost, say, £5 million to make or acquire, but that does *not* mean it is actually *worth* £5 million.

It is all very well for the accounts to state that stocks have been 'valued at the lower of cost and net realisable value', but if a film (or TV series) hasn't yet been screened, then how does anyone know if it will flop? Its 'realisable value' may only be £1 million – or, it could be considerably more than the £5 million it cost to make.

The same can be true of all sorts of other 'stocks' – from new toys to other manufactured goods. They may have cost a lot to acquire or make, but if the company hasn't fully started its advertising campaign to sell them, then how do they know that people will pay a good price for them, and that the stocks won't have to be drastically reduced in price (even to below cost price) in order to get rid of them?

Unfortunately, even the Notes to the Accounts may well not reveal the full extent of all sorts of perfectly legal 'creative accountancy' which has been known to give a misleading impression as to the state and worth of a company.

Financial Figures

Look at the figures.

Has the value of 'stocks' greatly increased since the previous year – but the company's turnover not shown a sizeable increase? If so, does this mean that the company is stockpiling its products ready for a major promotional sales effort – or is the company finding that sales are more difficult?

Has the figure for debtors greatly increased? Could this mean that one or more of the company's major customers is experiencing difficulties and is now a 'slow payer', or might eventually not be able to pay at all?

Have the earnings per share shown an increase over the previous year? Have the net assets increased? Is there any indication that the assets per share are worth considerably more than the share price?

Does the company have over-valued or under-valued assets? For example, perhaps the last reported valuation of a property was done some years ago and it would be reasonable to expect that its value has changed since then. Or perhaps the report contains a statement along the lines that 'in the opinion of the directors' the company's properties have 'an open market value substantially in excess of book value'. Could this attract a predator? Will the directors eventually make these assets 'sweat' and produce increased profits, or will they sell some of the property to realise some cash for expansion and other purposes?

Sometimes, as you struggle with the figures (and their notes) you may feel that the Financial Director must have been appointed for his flexibility. Perhaps the Chief Executive, when presented with a selection of accountants for possible hire, asked each of them: 'What is two plus three?'

Those who answered 'Five' were shown the door; those who asked 'Are you buying or selling?' were offered a lesser job in sales-contracts; and the one who said: 'What would you like me to make it?' was the one that got appointed Financial Director.

Even though there is considerable standardization of financial information in company reports, some companies may still, for some items, use different methods of 'creative accounting' from other companies. Watch out for it.

Directors And Management

A company report is also useful in assessing the abilities and character of the directors and senior management.

Is the report full of colour photos of the company's executives? Does it matter if the chairman has a pot belly – unless the company is involved in a health business? Or perhaps some of the other executives appear to have 'shifty eyes' – or maybe their contact lenses are uncomfortable?

Of course, if you are a psychologist, you could try to assess from the photos of the executives whether or not they have been recruited (or promoted) on the basis of what they look like, rather than how good they might be at their job. If the Chief Executive believes in 'teamwork' and is an ardent rugby player/American football fanatic, see if he has recruited a team that looks as if all its members are more suited to the sports field than to the business field. As I'm not a psychologist, all I can do is just speculate...

How many shares in the company do its directors own? Have their shareholdings increased or decreased since the previous year? I prefer to invest in companies where even the non-executive directors have demonstrated their confidence in the future of the company by buying some of its shares.

Don't be put off investing in a company if you discover that its Chief Executive is paid a fortune: he may well deserve it if he founded the company and/or it has performed extremely well, or he has accomplished a tremendously favourable turn-round in the company's fortunes.

There are many excellent executives, but also look out for those who appear to be more interested in their own pay, perks and prestige than in making sure that the company performs extremely well for shareholders.

The report will include a list of the company's directors. Do you know anything about them? What are their qualifications and experience? How long have they been with the company? The report may tell you hardly anything about them – or it may tell you more than you want to know! It depends on the company concerned. (Further consideration of company directors is given on pages 105-107 in the next chapter.)

Substantial Shareholdings

Does the annual report reveal any new substantial shareholders, or increases in the numbers of shares owned by existing
major shareholders? If so, then could these eventually lead to
a take-over bid by one of the companies concerned, or perhaps the shareholdings might be sold to another company
which might then make a bid?

Looking For Value

There are all sorts of 'value' approaches to investing. But when
I look at a company report I am especially trying to discover:

1. What is there about the company that makes it stand
    out from any competitors?
2. What is there that might justify a marked increase in
    the share price over the medium to long term?

As evidence of value in a company I would include:

(a) It operates in a niche industry where it can dominate
     its markets – or at least shows superiority of product,
     flexibility and pricing over its competitors.
(b) It has under-valued brand-names and/or reputation.
(c) It has assets worth more than its current share price.
(d) It has relatively little or no debt.
(e) Its price-earnings ratio is not more than the average
     for its market sector and/or the market as a whole.
(f) Its profits are soundly based on its continuing busi-
     nesses rather than enhanced by 'one off' deals which
     are unlikely to be repeated.
(g) It has quality management. The directors demonstrate
     that they have sufficient vision to plan properly for the
     long-term future and development of the company.

Annual General Meeting

The annual report will usually give the date of the company's Annual General Meeting. What is on the Agenda?

Will the directors be seeking shareholders' approval to change the articles and rules of the company in a way that might be detrimental to the shareholders' best interests?

Are they seeking in some way to make the company 'bid proof'?

Are the directors proposing to start or amend an executive share option scheme that you think might be too generous to the executives concerned?

Consider carefully the various agenda items. Is a particular director (whom you think is useless) seeking re-election to the board? If you disagree with any of the proposals, then use your proxy card to vote against them – or turn up at the meeting and express your views as well as vote. But don't always be negative. If the company is doing well, the management is excellent, and the proposals at the AGM are fair and reasonable, then vote in their favour.

The company *belongs* to its *owners* – the *shareholders.* The company is supposed to be run with their benefit in mind. Use your vote as one of the *owners* of the company.

Chapter 5:

What To Look For In A New Issue

British privatization issues awakened the interest of millions of people in filling in coupons in newspapers, sending off a cheque, and hoping that they had become investors in a 'new issue'. It seemed easy and, by buying shares in this way, they avoided having to pay any broker's buying commission.

However, not all new issues are successful (some are disastrous) and, of those that do succeed, some fare far better than others. So what do I look for in a new issue?

How Are The Shares Being Sold?

There are various ways of bringing new issue shares to market: by a fixed price offer, tender offer, mixed issue, placing, and by an introduction.

Introduction

An introduction is most commonly used by overseas companies that want their shares listed on the London Stock Market. Such companies may well already have their shares quoted on the stock market of their 'home' country, but feel that a London listing would add to the marketability of the company's shares, perhaps demonstrate that the company has international interests, and possibly also add to the prestige of the company.

Various market makers agree to 'make a market' in the shares in London and thus make the shares available to the UK public. Usually, no 'new' shares are issued.

Whenever I read about a forthcoming introduction I look carefully at the background of the company concerned. Is it likely to use its appearance on the London market as a prelude to a take-over bid (perhaps a few years later) for a British company? If so, what are its possible bid targets? The potential 'targets', over a period of years, might then prove a more rewarding investment than the company coming to the London market!

Placing

Placings can sometimes be extremely profitable for those lucky enough to be able to participate in them – but a number of placings in the UK are not 'open' to all private investors. This is because when a company decides to seek a placing, the company and its advisers set a price for the shares and then the shares are 'placed' mainly with City institutions, pension funds, and very wealthy private investors.

However, if you read of a company coming to the market via a placing, and you feel attracted to it, then ask your broker if he can get you some shares: occasionally, you might be successful, especially if your broker is the sponsor to the placing.

Fixed Price Offer

Many new issues come to the market by means of a fixed price offer: the shares are available at a set, fixed price. This makes the value of the company fairly easy to ascertain, and it becomes easier for an investor to make a judgment as to whether or not it might prove to be a worthwhile investment for him.

If so many people apply for shares that applications are received for many more shares than are being offered, then they may find their application is 'scaled down' and they receive only a small proportion of the shares for which they applied (plus a cheque for the remainder of their application money); or an investor may find that his share application form is put in a ballot and he may then receive no shares at all (and his cheque is returned), or he may receive all the shares he applied for, or he may receive only a proportion of the shares applied for, plus a cheque for the balance. It all depends on the terms of the offer.

Tender Offer

Tender offers can take different forms, and it is vital that investors in such offers carefully read the terms of the offer in order to avoid making very expensive mistakes.

Sometimes, the issuing house for the offer sets a minimum price for the shares and invites investors to apply for them and state what amount they are prepared to pay, per share, for their investment.

For example, the issuer could state that the minimum price is 100p per share. Some investors may think that the shares are worth 110p each. Others may be prepared to pay 105p or 120p or even 130p.

The issuer examines all the offers for the shares and then sets a 'striking price' – perhaps 115p per share. Anyone who applied for shares at 115p or any price above 115p, receives all (or part) of the shareholding he applied for, but only pays 115p per share – even if he offered to pay, say, 118p per share. Anyone who offered less than the 115p striking price receives no shares at all and his money is refunded.

Not all tender offers work in this way, as some investors have found out in a painful and expensive way. The issuer of the shares might invite tenders for shares at prices above 100p per share. Some people are really enthusiastic about the company concerned and each offer to buy, say, 2,500 shares at 135p per share. Other people offer 120p, or 105p and other varying amounts over 100p. The issuer then accepts the highest offers at the price they offered.

This might mean that the average price offered was only 110p, so that when the shares have their 'first day of deal-ings' perhaps deals in them are only done at prices around 110p – 115p. Yet the people who offered 135p for the shares have had their offers accepted at 135p – they are thus immediately showing a loss on their investment.

If you are in doubt about the exact terms of a tender offer, don't be afraid to ask your stockbroker or other investment adviser to explain them to you clearly: it could well save you money.

Mixed Issue

A mixed issue is where the number of new shares on offer is split into two categories: some are offered at a fixed price, while the remainder are open to tender offers at or above that fixed price.

For such issues it pays to double-check your application before sending it in, just to make quite sure that everything has been correctly completed as mixed issues can sometimes have rather confusing application forms.

What To Look For In The Prospectus

Many people cannot be bothered to wade through pages of small print in a new issue prospectus. Sometimes, they are attracted to invest in a new issue by a lot of marketing and publicity hype; or by the sheer ease of simply filling in a coupon and sending off a cheque.

Just because a company has a familiar name does not mean that the price being asked for its shares is reasonable: the people selling the shares may, perhaps, be asking for a bit too much because they are greedy, or have been poorly advised by their merchant bankers and other advisers. Or a sudden change in market conditions can make the offer price unattractive.

I ignore many new issues. Some are over-priced. Others are for companies whose businesses do not appeal to me: perhaps they are in industries with considerable and greatly increasing competition, or are involved in commodities of which there might soon be a glut which could possibly lead to a dramatic drop in prices and consequently a decline in company profitability.

Is the new issue fully-paid or partly-paid? If the full cost of the shares is not payable immediately, then will you have sufficient funds readily available to meet the next payment on them – or do you hope to sell the shares at a profit before making the second payment?

For the new issues that do attract my further attention, I look for the following:

1.   What is the company's likely p/e ratio? If it is much higher than other companies in its sector then it has to demonstrate clearly why it should command a premium price, otherwise I am not interested in it.

2.   What percentage of the company is being made

available in the new issue? Who will continue to own large shareholdings in it? If the company looks as if it will remain controlled by foreign interests, then this can sometimes be a 'turn off'.

3. What happens to the money being raised by the new issue? Does most of it go to the directors and founders of the company selling many of their shares? Does a large part of it go to paying off debts? How much of it will be used for expansion purposes?

If it looks as if the directors and founders might be 'selling out', then this could deter me from investing if the company did not still retain some good, committed, motivated management.

I do not mind company founders reaping perhaps millions of pounds reward from a new issue for all their hard work in creating the company: they deserve it if the company has been built up successfully. But I would hope that the founders would still retain a reasonable share stake – if only to help motivate them to ensure the continuing success of the company.

A company having a new issue mainly to pay off debt does not appeal to me at all.

Apart from privatization issues, the strongest appeal (to me, at least) comes from companies that clearly specify in their prospectus the exact purposes to which the proceeds of the new issue will be put – ideally, to fund a new factory extension, or further enhance the production capabilities of the company, or to fund expansion in the same or related activities to the company's existing business.

4. What is the asset value per share of the company? How does this compare with the price at which the company's shares are being sold?

I like companies where the share price is close to the asset value per share – at least this means that the 'downside' has some reasonable limits. Of course, in some industries (like advertising and other 'people-related' businesses) the net tangible asset value might be low and it would be reasonable to expect a premium to be paid for the intangible value of the creative staff, etc. – so long as it is clear from the prospectus that their contracts of employment make it unattractive for them to walk away from the company or do anything which could be harmful to the company.

A premium might also be expected for companies that are clearly in thriving industries and where the return on their assets could be considerable.

5. Who are the directors of the company? What are their qualifications? How long have they been with the company? What are their terms of employment?

I am wary of companies that appoint as chairman, shortly before their flotation, a member of the nobility who has little or no experience of business. Why do they think they need the supposed 'respectability' of a knight or lord: isn't their business and its management respectable enough in its own right? Of course, many members of the nobility are highly respectable and their place in certain boardrooms (as chairman or non-executive or executive directors) can be extremely helpful to the companies concerned, particularly if they have useful contacts or can bring a particular expertise to the business. But it has been known for a few companies to recruit a member of the nobility purely to add a 'gloss' to a rather undistinguished business that has subsequently performed very poorly.

If you are not sure about some of the qualification abbreviation letters listed at the end of a director's name,

then look them up. Some people put after their names
letters that simply demonstrate that they have paid a
subscription fee to join a particular organization, not that
they have passed an examination.

Letters after people's names may well demonstrate that
they are respectable, have passed examinations, or are otherwise qualified in a particular occupation or activity – it does
not necessarily follow that they are particularly intelligent
or can run a business successfully.

Some of the best businesses in the world were founded
and are run successfully by people with no formal qualifications. Other companies have appalling track records, show
poor returns on investors' funds, produce sluggish or falling
profits, etc., and yet may have a board stuffed with accountants and dignitaries. An accountant can count – he may not
necessarily know how to create and run a thriving business.
It is interesting to reflect that the UK produces more
accountants than Japan or Germany.

Carefully read any details in the prospectus about the
previous employment history of the directors and management. Were the companies they worked for successful at the
time they were employed by them?

Companies that have only just recruited a proper management team might experience some 'teething problems',
unless the people concerned have worked together elsewhere. It has been known for new management to have
fierce arguments amongst themselves to the detriment of
the company.

Are the terms of employment of the directors too generous? Do they provide a proper incentive for the directors
to increase profits and produce good returns for the
investors?

I dislike companies that pay huge basic salaries to directors:
pay should be closely linked to performance. I am also wary

of companies that might ill-reward certain excellent directors and other senior management who might then walk out of the company, taking many of the company's clients with them, or otherwise establishing a strong, rival organization that could seriously harm the company's future prospects.

6. Who is sponsoring the issue? What other professional firms (solicitors, accountants, etc.) are involved with the issue?

Perhaps you have experience of a particular firm of solicitors which you found were rather incompetent or took ages to do anything; or know of a firm of accountants that is perhaps more willing than some other firms to turn a 'blind eye' to certain things and relies heavily on 'directors' assurances' – in which case you will probably wish to avoid new issues in which such firms are involved.

7. What is hidden away in the small print? Are there any outstanding legal actions which could seriously affect the company? Have any of the directors previously run businesses that have collapsed or otherwise gone into liquidation? If so, I would not be particularly keen to participate in the new issue.

Do any of the directors own large shareholdings in other companies with which the company does business and which might, perhaps, lead to a conflict of interest?

8. What is the profit record of the company – and what is the profits forecast? If the profit record is somewhat erratic, are you happy with the explanations (if any) given for this? (See also Chapter 4: *What To Look For In A Company Report.*)

9. Do you have any personal knowledge of the company whose shares are being offered? For example, having travelled extensively in the US, I knew that competition amongst cookie sellers in that country was tremendous. I was therefore somewhat doubtful about the prospects of a fairly small US cookie company when it first came to the UK Stock Market.

I read the prospectus and saw that the company's prospective price-earnings ratio was far too high, especially as it was possible at that time to buy shares in a major UK biscuit manufacturer instead at a much lower rating. The major UK company also had considerable assets, produced good profits, and had take-over possibilities. What, then, justified the US company's high p/e?

The prospectus also revealed that the US company had opened a London shop and so my wife and I visited the store. Not only did the cookies not appeal to us, but the product range seemed rather narrow.

We stood outside the store for ten minutes and during that time no customers entered the store. Maybe we had picked the wrong time on the wrong day? Maybe with a good publicity campaign people would flock to the store? Maybe we were in a minority in not liking the majority of the cookies on offer?

We decided not to take a chance. 'When in doubt – stay out' – so we did not subscribe for the US cookie company's shares. This saved us a lot of money as within two years the share price fell to below half, and subsequently fell even further.

Press Comment

Before investing in a new issue, read as much press comment about the issue as possible. You may find that different financial columnists have different views on the merits of a particular issue – or they may all recommend it and yet the issue still proves to be a flop.

Press comment is useful at highlighting certain aspects of the prospectus which you might have overlooked, or perhaps a journalist has discovered things that are not in the prospectus, but which could seriously affect the company's chances of success: perhaps the managing director is facing a costly divorce action that will force him to sell more shares in the company which might depress the share price? Or maybe one of the directors has associates that have been involved in various illegal activities. Or perhaps the company's products are soon to come under fierce competition from a low-cost foreign competitor.

Use the press comment as a balance against which to weigh your own views of the new issue concerned.

Timing Details

With some new issues, all share applications are treated equally if they have arrived by a specified date. Investors can then, if they wish, wait until the last possible moment before sending in their share applications, just in case economic or political circumstances or some other event might have affected the prospects of the company concerned and lead to the issue being a financial disaster for the private investor.

It is also advisable to check with your broker as to the likely chances of success for the new issue *just before* sending in your application. He may know some market gossip and advise that the issue is likely to be under subscribed and a flop, and so an application would not be worthwhile. Or he may say the application looks like being a success.

Some new issues are sold on a 'first come, first served'

basis: a specified closing date is given for applications, but this is accompanied by a statement that the offer to subscribe for shares will close immediately applications for all the shares on offer have been received. Such a closure of the offer might then take place well before the formal specified 'latest' closing date.

Make sure that, however you decide to apply for new issue shares, you take account of possible postal vagaries and delays. A number of people like to hand in personally their applications to the issue's sponsors (or the sponsor's agents) just to be sure that their application has definitely been received in time.

Ballot Problems

Some new issues are heavily over-subscribed and so there is a ballot for scaled-down applications. For example, someone who applied for 5,000 shares at £1 per share might be unsuccessful in the ballot and so not receive any shares, or he might be successful – but only be sold 500 shares instead of the 5,000 for which he had applied.

An investor receiving only 500 shares – even if the shares immediately went to a premium of 3p or so per share – might well find that if he sells the shares he will do so at a loss because dealing costs will have eaten up all his profit. His £5,000 cheque will have been cashed, and it might be as long as two weeks or so before he receives the £4,500 balance of his money, during which time, of course, he has lost the interest which he might have earned if the money had remained in his own bank account.

Therefore, if you are hoping for 'quick profits' – but feel that a new issue might involve a considerable scaling back in your application – then carefully consider whether or not it is worth the bother and expense of applying.

Sometimes, people have been tempted to borrow heavily in order to apply for shares which they cannot really afford, hoping that they might be allocated a reasonable number of shares in the ballot and that the shares will command a considerable premium on the first day of dealings. This can be dangerous. Suppose something dramatic happens just before the issue deadline and the issue is a flop and the shares then trade at less than their issue price: could the investor comfortably bear such a loss?

Even if an issue is successful, but an investor's application for, say 100,000 shares is scaled back to 10,000 – will the interest costs on his borrowing wipe out all his profits if it takes two weeks for the balance cheque to arrive?

You *can* increase your chances of success in a ballot. For example, if you can afford 5,000 shares, why not apply for 2,500 in your own name and get your spouse to apply for 2,500 in her name: at least that way you stand two chances instead of one in actually being allocated some shares.

What Do You Really Want From A New Issue?

Finally, before investing in a new issue, examine carefully the reasons why you want to invest in it. If you are investing in the hope of selling the shares at a profit within a few weeks, then are you sure that you will not be placed in an embarrassing financial position if, for some reason, the shares do not go to a premium? After dealing costs, you might then show a loss if you sold the shares within weeks of buying them. If you are in any doubt as to whether or not the shares will reach a premium, then maybe it is safest only to invest money which you will not need until the shares *do* show you a profit?

Or maybe you are investing for the medium-to-long-term,

as you believe the company has excellent prospects for profits, growth, and a rising share price.

Whatever your reason for investing, try to disregard all the hype surrounding new issues and only invest if you feel confident in your investment: if in doubt, keep out! But still remember that *some* new issues can prove to be very profitable.

Chapter 6:

How To Find Take-Over Targets

It used to be that huge, multi-national corporations were 'safe' from take-overs. Sometimes, such companies agreed to a merger with other companies, but there were very few contested take-overs. However, with the advent of junk bonds, all sorts of 'financial engineering', and with financial institutions willing to lend vast sums of money, the only companies that appeared 'safe' from 'attack' were those protected from take-over by a government and/or by legal and political conditions in the countries in which they operated, or they were protected by their share structures or the company rules which they had adopted, perhaps many years ago when they were first incorporated.

With so many companies now open to 'attack', it has become much more difficult to predict which companies will be the most likely ones to receive take-over bids.

Nowadays, it is not only a full take-over bid from another company that can make a share price soar – sometimes the results are even better, longer-term, if new management arrives at the company by buying a large share stake in it.

This chapter will therefore use the word 'take-over' to mean both a full take-over of a whole company, and a 'take-over' by new management buying a large shareholding but without acquiring the whole company.

113

Take-Over Target Characteristics

I have made a reasonable amount of money finding bid targets, buying the shares of such companies, and then waiting for a bid and accepting the best take-over terms.

How do I find likely take-over targets? I look for one or more of the following characteristics in a company:

1. Another company, or small group of 'connected' companies, already owns a fairly large shareholding in it.

2. It has assets worth considerably more than its share price and a management (or members of a family owning a large share stake) who might be persuaded to 'do a deal' so that they can realize the full value of their investment.

3. It has a low capitalization, a full stock market quotation, and might be suitable as a 'shell' company into which a person or company can inject new assets and then build up the company.

4. It is in an area of activity where its p/e ratio is relatively low compared with its competitors so that a rival could reduce its own p/e by taking it over.

5. It has under-valued 'brand names' that could attract a company that hopes to exploit those brand names more fully; or the company has a number of subsidiaries which, if they were sold off, could attract large sums of money so that the 'parts' of the company prove to be worth more than the 'whole'. There are a number of entrepreneurs who have made fortunes as 'break up merchants', buying companies and then selling off some or all of their assets for sums which considerably exceed their purchase costs of the companies concerned.

6. It has an elderly chairman and/or managing director/ chief executive, or the company has a generally 'old' board of directors and management succession is unclear.

7. It is in some other way a 'special situation'. For example, if a company is family controlled, a 'family squabble' could lead to a 'break up' in the family interests and perhaps even to an invitation to various take-over bidders to make an offer for some of the family shareholdings.

Take-over bidders also seem to like companies that have fallen on hard times, which have already carried out major re-structuring and are on the point of a good 'turn around', but where the share price has largely ignored this, thus leaving a predator an opportunity to make a bid and then claim the 'turn around' as his own work!

Take-Over Examples: Share Stakes

My wife once bought shares in a chain of newsagents for 150p per share because we had read in a newspaper that an insurance company owned 17 per cent of it. To us, this seemed somewhat unusual. UK insurance companies do not generally have stakes as large as 17 per cent in such a company. The insurance company concerned was at that time under some pressure to merge with another company. We therefore thought that its 17 per cent stake in the newsagents might well be sold to a potential bidder.

Within three months, another company made a bid for the newsagents and my wife accepted their cash offer of 210p per share.

The easiest way to spot possible take-over targets is to

look for small companies where a major company in the same line of business already has a large share stake.

For example, I once bought shares in a small quarrying company because a larger company, which had interests in similar activities, owned 29.37 per cent of it.

The shares cost me 77p each, but I was able to sell them in less than a year for 152p each when the major company launched its take-over bid.

However, not all stakes held by large companies in smaller ones lead to the large companies bidding for them – they may, instead, accept a take-over offer for their share stake from another company. It can also require patience before anything happens.

For example, I once bought shares in a company for 35p each in the hope that a major company, which owned 29.9 per cent of it, would eventually either launch a bid for the whole company or sell its share stake to another bidder. Nothing much happened for more than 18 months – and then a completely different company made a bid for it and I accepted their cash offer of 113p per share.

Another example was when I bought shares in a small packaging and investment company in the hope that another company, which owned a large shareholding in it, would either use that shareholding as a 'springboard' for a bid, or might sell the shareholding to an entrepreneur who could then move into the company as it was small enough to be used as a 'shell' into which he could put further activities and generally expand it.

The shares in the small company cost me 12.5p each. The share price did not move very much until, almost four years later, entrepreneurs moved into the company. I eventually sold most of my shares in it for 205p each five years after I had acquired them.

Strategic Share Stakes

It should be stressed that some companies hold 'strategic' share stakes in other companies to *protect* them from being taken over. Perhaps they do this to ensure that the company concerned remains a good customer for their products, or perhaps there are family or historical reasons why two companies should enjoy a close relationship without one company taking control of the other.

Therefore, do *not* just buy shares in a company *solely* because another company owns a large shareholding in it. You may find that this strategic shareholding effectively *stops* a take-over bid. Find out how long the company concerned has held its strategic share stake: is it likely to be held for 'defensive' or 'offensive' purposes?

Are there any special circumstances that could lead to a bid? Perhaps the company owning the share stake may need some funds for its own expansion plans and so could be persuaded to sell the share stake to another company. Or maybe the company has new management that might like to carry out a 'tidying up' operation by either selling off the share-stake or using it as a platform from which to launch a take-over bid.

Price-Earnings Levels

I do *not* invest in companies that have high p/es, buoyed up by bid hopes. The bid may never happen and the share price may drop rapidly as bid hopes fade. I prefer companies with p/es at or around their sector average, which means that any bid prospects are really 'thrown in for free', and hopefully the companies concerned will still perform well even without any bids.

Mergers/Entrepreneurs

Another bid example was when I bought shares in a small engineering company for 17p each. It had a relatively low capitalization (12.5 million shares), reasonable assets, and one family held more than 20 per cent of the shares. I hoped the company would appeal to a private engineering company wanting to do a reverse take-over and thus acquire a Stock Market quotation.

Within 2½ years it was announced that the company was to merge with another engineering company and I was able to sell my shares for a reasonable profit.

In the case of mergers and/or entrepreneurs moving into a company, I always wait to assess what impact this will have on the shares before selling them. For example, I once bought shares in a small company for 50p each as I thought that a family which had a large stake in it might eventually be interested in a take-over bid.

Within two years another company acquired a significant part of the family's shareholding and new directors were appointed to the small company. The shares went up on this news, but I waited for more than six months before I sold some of the shares: for 165p each. The market had by then decided to re-rate the company as a result of its new management and their plans for the company's future.

Sometimes, when I have invested in a small company, hoping that someone will be attracted to its quoted status and will build on this by injecting new assets into the company, what has happened instead is that the whole company has been taken over and it has lost its full Stock Market quotation.

For example, I bought shares in a small company for 35p each because, despite its size, it had interests in gravel extraction, pre-cast concrete products, oil distribution and civil engineering. It also operated a hotel on the Isle of Wight and manufactured holdalls and toiletries. The company's profits record had been respectable, but the company had a low capitalization, and it seemed to me that it was ripe for a take-over or it could, perhaps, be 'broken up' with its various subsidiaries being sold off, with the cash proceeds being distributed to shareholders.

Within a year, a larger company made a recommended bid for the company. I accepted their bid offer of 60p per share, having earlier that same month sold half my shareholding in the market for 61p per share.

Selling Too Soon

Not all my 'bid hopes' investments in small companies have been successful. Some such companies in which I have investments have still to succumb to a take-over approach, while in a few cases I have recognized the take-over potential but sold too soon, either because I needed the released investment funds for other purposes, or because I was too impatient for a take-over to happen and decided to sell my investment.

For example, I bought shares in a chain of High Street jewellery retailers for 80p per share. The firm's directors and their families owned a very large share stake in the company. It had reasonable assets and profits record, but I felt that the jewellery retail market at that time was becoming increasingly competitive and so perhaps the company might be the subject of a take-over bid. I also thought it might attract the attention of someone who could possibly inject further assets into the company and use the benefits of its full share quotation to expand the company rapidly by having rights issues to raise the necessary funds for further company purchases and/or by issuing new shares as part of the take-over terms for other companies.

Nothing much happened to the share price, and I did not hear of any bid rumours.

Nine months later I was concerned about the market for shares in that company and I thought a bid for it would be some years away and that the company's share price would not move much in the meantime. I sold the shares for 78p each.

You can imagine how I felt when, the following year, another company bid 250p per share for it!

This emphasizes, yet again, that it's not possible to 'win them all'. No investor, with a reasonable sized share port-folio, can get it right 100 per cent of the time. Losses and 'missed opportunities' just have to be accepted as part of the game as long as, overall, reasonable profits are still made from share trading. But at least the jewellery chain experi-ence taught me to be a bit more patient . . .

Companies To Avoid

Sometimes, take-overs can be useful pointers as to which companies should be avoided. The company which paid 250p per share for a jewellery chain appeared to me to be paying rather a high price: would the bidding company manage to make any profits from it?

The successful bidder eventually experienced some diffi-culties and its share price plunged.

Therefore, use take-over bids to examine not only the company being taken over, but also the company making the bid. Any sign that a company is paying too much, or expanding too rapidly by take-overs on borrowed money, could well be a sign to avoid its shares – although they may power ahead during all the bid activity, a few years later the problems may reveal themselves.

Timing

Sometimes, it pays to sell a share if take-over hopes look some way off, and then buy back into the company when take-over rumours look more solid.

For example, I bought shares in a small company which manufactured swimwear and sound reproduction equipment. The shares cost me 19p each.

The company had a full Stock Market quotation and its directors and their families held a large share stake in it. I thought the company might either attract a take-over approach, or that someone might pay a good price just for the swimwear division.

When I felt that bid hopes had faded, I sold the shares for 22p each within a year from their purchase. I invested the sales proceeds elsewhere.

However, I still believed that one day something might happen that would make the company's share price soar – so I kept track of the company and collected press cuttings on it.

Five-and-a-half years later, my wife bought shares in the company for 30p each and increased her shareholding (paying 39p per share) four months later.

Within a year it was announced that the president of the company (who was 84) had sold a large part of his shareholding and that a City investing group had acquired 29.9 per cent of the company for 55p per share. A member of that group became chief executive and two other members also joined the board. The shares, of course, were able to be sold in the market for 55p each.

Fun and profits can also be had with larger companies.

For example, my wife bought shares in a department stores group at a time when we felt that British High Street retailing was in the middle of a 'shake up' and the company concerned looked vulnerable to a bid. Sure enough, later that same year, another company made a successful take-over bid and my wife made some excellent profits.

I have also made some very good gains from a number of my overseas investments, when the companies concerned have been the subject of take-over bids.

Assets

Again, it is worth repeating that I only buy shares in take-over targets that have solid assets. That way, hopefully, the 'downside risk' is limited. If a bid does not happen, the company concerned should still be able to generate reasonable profits, or sell off some of its assets and thus maintain a realistic share price level.

Solid assets and reasonable dividends allow an investor to hold on to a share even if bid hopes start to grow dim. With a share price mainly supported by bid hopes (rather than assets), if the bid hopes fade, an investor might have to act very quickly and dump the shares before they plummet. Sometimes, it may not be possible to jump in time.

When I bought shares in a major producer of basic electrical products I did so not only because the company seemed to me to be a likely take-over target, but its products were in almost every British household and the company had solid assets. The shares cost me 288p each.

Two years later, I was getting a bit bored with this investment. No bidder had appeared. But the dividend yield was reasonable, the company still had excellent assets and good products. Its price-earnings ratio was still modest. I therefore held on to the shares.

Within a year, I thought again about selling my shares as at that time I felt the market had risen too high, too fast, and I was concerned about a possible major correction in the market. However, I thought the company's shares had not been influenced too much by the frenzy of the market, although they were by now over 540p each.

Soon after, a major company made a bid for the company which was 'topped' by a rival bidder before the first bidder increased its offer to 700p per share and its bid succeeded.

Trend Spotting

Spotting trends can also lead to handsome profits from take-over bids. For example, when one Japanese company took over a well-known upmarket UK clothes manufacturer and retailer I thought it would not be too long before another Japanese company did the same. I therefore benefited when another UK company of a somewhat similar nature in which I had shares was subsequently taken over by the Japanese.

Take-Over Surprises

Sometimes, my wife and I have bought shares in a company for its growth prospects, strength of management, or for some other reason, and a take-over bid has come as a complete surprise to us.

For example, my wife bought shares in a property group for 69p per share. We were both impressed by the quality design of its buildings and new office and industrial developments. We believed that good design makes a building last longer, and attracts quality tenants willing to pay high rents. The company also had excellent management.

Within eighteen months from my wife's purchase of the

shares, another property group made a bid for the company and she accepted their cash terms of 135p per share.

Where To Find Take-Over Indicators

The *Corporate Register* and *Company Refs*, both published by HS Financial Publishing, are good places to start if you want to find details of large shareholders in various companies and the percentage of shares owned by the directors. Also, look out for news items regarding newly acquired or increased share stakes in companies: could these have been bought as a prelude to a bid?

Both the *Corporate Register* and *Company Refs* – and the *Financial Times* share price pages – provide details of companies' capitalizations. This information is helpful in assessing which companies are small enough to have 'shell' potential.

Sometimes, the 'trading volume' of a company's shares might indicate that a bid may be on the way. For example, if lots of shares have recently changed hands (far more than on a 'normal' day of trading) *and* the share price has remained firm, or gone up, then this can, on occasion, indicate that a bid may be on the way, or that a particular investor may soon reveal a large share stake in the company.

The trading volume of some leading British shares is given in a number of newspapers, including the *Financial Times*. More detailed figures can be purchased from the Stock Exchange.

Carefully watch the share price of a company which you think might be a bid target. Does the share price remain firm, or go up, when most other companies in the same sector have weak or falling share prices? Does the share price rise, fall back a bit, then rise again, and keep following that pattern for several weeks, but each time the 'rising price' is higher than before? This could be the result of a would-be predator and his advisers 'testing the market': they buy some shares in the bid target and see how much their buying causes the price to rise. They then sell some shares with two objects in mind: (a) to try to find out how far the shares will fall if they are not buying them; and (b) to try to see who buys the shares that they are selling – is there a possible rival bidder for the company? They then buy even more shares in the company and repeat the pattern of buying a lot and selling some.

I would stress that none of these observations is fool-proof: sometimes they may indicate potential take-over activity – many times they will give misleading signs and no take-over will appear.

If you want to find companies with elderly directors whom you think might be amenable to a bid approach (or whose death might cause the company to attract a bidder) then scan the newspapers for 'profile' interviews of company directors. If you like the take-over potential of a particular company and have already obtained a copy of its annual report and just wish to check the ages of one or more of the company's directors, then visit your local reference library. There are a number of 'corporate registers', professional directories and works like *Who's Who* and *People of Today* which might include biographical details of the people in whom you are interested.

Treat with caution 'tips' in newspapers (especially in the Sunday newspapers) about possible take-over bids. You will be reading of the 'tip' at the same time as millions of other people and the market makers will probably mark up the shares concerned in anticipation of a rush of buyers. You could find yourself at the end of a queue of buyers, paying a very high price for shares which might possibly plummet if a large shareholder decides to take advantage of the share price rise and sell out and/or the bid fails to materialize.

This is not to say that newspaper 'tips' should be completely ignored – but use your own judgment (and also that of your broker) before buying the 'tipped' shares: are there any signs, other than the newspaper 'tip', that a bid is on the way? How good is the track record of the writer giving the 'tip'? Some writers are excellent at spotting bid targets – others are pretty hopeless.

Be even more careful of internet bulletin boards. Some of the gossip on them might be from people who bought the 'tipped' shares some time ago and are now showing a loss on their investment: the only way they can get out at a profit is to convince enough people that a bid is about to take place so that they all rush in and buy the shares, forcing the share price upwards. The 'tipper' then sells his shares at a profit, while most of the other investors are stuck with shares in a company that may never receive a bid and the share price may then start a rapid downward slide.

If you are interested in a particular company, but have not yet invested in it, then get a copy of its latest Report – or look for such details on its website. From the Report and Accounts you might be able to discover if the company is a 'turn round' possibility, or if it has undervalued assets. It should also reveal details of the directors' shareholdings and any investors who own a very substantial holding in the company. (See Chapter 4: *What To Look For In A Company Report.*)

What To Do In The Event Of A Bid

Suppose you have invested in a company that has attracted a take-over bid: what should you do? Accept the offer? Sell in the market in case the bid fails?

The best thing to do is to be patient. Read the details of the take-over offer carefully. Note the deadline for the acceptance of the offer. Do *not* immediately accept the take-over terms: the first offer may not be the best.

For example, one year, on 24th November, a company in which I had a shareholding, became the object of a take-over bid at 550p per share. An investor could have decided to take a good profit and sell the shares in the market at around that price. It would have been foolish to have done so, because on 7th December that year another company offered 660p per share. The first bidder then offered 700p – an increase of 150p per share on its original offer.

It is quite often best to delay accepting any bid until the last possible moment, taking into account any likely vagaries and delays within the postal system.

Read as much press comment as possible: is the bid likely to succeed? Will the offer be increased? Are there any likely rival bidders? Will the bid 'target' produce excellent profits forecasts that demonstrate its superiority over the bidder? If the bid fails, what will happen to the 'target's share price – will it fall? If so, by how much? Is the bid likely to be 'blocked' by the Government or by other political or legal action?

If Government, or other political action, may delay or prevent a successful bid, then sell your shares if you feel that their price will fall dramatically without a successful bid.

Are there strong indications that a rival bidder may appear and offer a higher price? For example, perhaps a company has had a share stake in the 'target' for some time and held 'merger discussions' with the 'target' company, or perhaps a company has a trading relationship with the 'target' which it wishes to protect and so might be per-suaded to launch a rival bid for the 'target'. If so, then you might consider buying more shares in the 'target' in the hope of benefiting from a higher rival bid, or perhaps from an increased offer from the original bidder.

Also remember: just because a bid is 'recommended'

**or 'accepted' by the board of the company, it does *not*
necessarily mean that the bid will be successful at that
level.** The board may only have a small shareholding and
institutional investors, with much larger holdings, may
not accept the original bid terms. The institutions may
hold out for an increased offer, or wait in the hope of a
rival bidder coming forward to make a much more generous bid.

Do not feel obliged to accept a bid, just because a bidder
is offering a bit more for your shares than they were immediately before the bid was announced. Perhaps the bidder is
aware of developments in the company that might be more
profitable to you if the 'target' continued as an independent
company? For example, maybe the 'target' is due to
announce a considerable increase in its profits, or a disposal
of a subsidiary or some property at a great profit, or perhaps
it has invented or discovered something that could have a
dramatic effect on its profits.

Questions

Why is the bidder making his bid? Is it to break up the
company and to use the proceeds to pay off the bidder's
own debts? If so, then why accept the bid? Surely the 'target'
could attract a more desirable bidder – or maybe even break
itself up to the benefit of its existing shareholders? Are the
bidder's own profits likely to suffer a downturn and so the
bidder is hoping to buy future growth and profits at a
'knockdown' price?

Can cost savings genuinely be made if the 'target' is taken
over? Has the 'target' failed to exploit its markets? Has it got
poor management that needs to be replaced by the bidding
company so that a successful bid will lead to the revitaliza-
tion of the company?

Sometimes, a bidder will offer shares in its own company as well as (or instead of) cash for the shares in the 'target' company. This can have tax implications and it is a good idea to ask your broker or accountant or other adviser as to which offer is the most financially attractive in your own particular circumstances.

If shares in the bidding company are offered, before you accept them consider at what price those shares might be at the time you want to sell them. Are they likely to drift downwards? Would you be better off selling your shares in the market and reinvesting your profits elsewhere?

Before accepting shares in the bidder's company, ask yourself if you would actually have *bought* shares in that company. If not, then why accept their shares in a bid?

If you mainly invest in the hope of finding take-over targets, then it would probably be best if you took cash or sold your shares in the market, since if you accepted the bidder's shares, it might be some time before the bidder itself was taken-over.

Suppose a bidder offers 150p per share and the shares in the market are quoted at 150p: should you sell in the market, or sell to the bidder? If you sell in the market, you will have to pay broker's commission, whereas if you sell to the bidder, then no commission will be deducted. But what is the timetable for payment?

Sometimes, it is more profitable to sell in the market and reinvest the cash immediately if you know of another excellent investment opportunity, rather than perhaps waiting weeks for the bidder's cheque to arrive. It may also be that there is little chance of a rival bid (or a higher offer from the bidder) and if this is the case, then it may well pay to sell quickly in the market rather than wait for the final deadline for the bid and then a further delay before payment is made.

Wanted

A take-over bid can make an investor actually feel *wanted*.
He may have held shares in a company for years, but been
provided with pathetic company reports showing a poor
company performance, received meagre dividends, and been
generally ignored at the Annual General Meeting. A hostile
bid allows him to 'get even' with the management that has
taken him for granted and treated him so badly: he can sell
his shares to the bidder and hope that the 'target' will be
taken-over and the 'target's' management then be slung out
– ideally, without compensation, although all too many
company directors and executives now manage to secure
generous 'golden parachutes' and heavy contractual 'depar-
ture' payments, even if their performance has been poor.

However, it may be that the 'target' has always treated its
shareholders well, kept them fully informed of its activities,
promptly answered any queries, paid reasonable dividends,
and the share price has been steadily rising: in which case,
should the investor remain loyal to the 'target' rather than
selling his shares to a predator?

This depends on how well he believes the 'target' will
perform if it is *not* taken over, and perhaps whether or not
he prefers a quick profit on a take-over, or a possibly much
larger profit in a number of years' time if the 'target'
remains independent, but develops to its full potential with
a possibly dramatic increase in its dividends and share price.

Take-over bids can be fun. Occasionally, the bidder will
even provide a free video cassette which gives some of the
reasons why it feels its bid should succeed.

Sometimes, there are a variety of bidders and the investor
is bombarded with take-over documents by every post.
Enjoy it! But don't be afraid to take profits where appropriate, and save them for reinvestment or other purposes.

Chapter 7:

A Right Worth Having?

Sometimes, a quoted company might ask its shareholders for more money by offering them shares in a rights issue. Each shareholder will have the *right* to buy a certain number of new shares in the company at a specified price.

For example, the company might offer a 1-for-5 rights issue: for every five shares already held by the shareholder, he gets a right to buy one more share. The rights issue can be on a 1-for-1 basis, or 1-for-3 basis, or all sorts of other variations.

Usually, at the time the rights issue is announced, the new shares are offered at a discount to the current price of the company's existing quoted shares. If the shares are quoted at 350p, perhaps the rights issue shares might be offered at, say, 310p each. This does not necessarily mean that the investor will make 40p per share profit from his rights issue shares.

The market makers, on hearing of the rights issue, might mark down the shares to, say, 345p each. Then, after the rights issue has taken place, the price may fall back to a price somewhere between 350p and 310p: say, 330p – it depends on investors' and market makers' views on the value of the shares now that there are more shares in issue.

Theoretically, the price should have fallen in accordance

with a mathematical formula based on the number of new shares issued, its percentage in relation to the number of 'old' shares, the respective prices of the shares, etc. Personally, while I feel that this does, of course, have a lot of impact on the price – it is still 'sentiment' that will finally decide the ex-rights price of the shares. The effect of the rights issue can be to 'wake up' existing shareholders (and others in the City) to the fact that the company is doing something: if the rights issue money is being used to fund an acquisition, then this might have a favourable impact on the company's share price, especially if the acquisition is considered to be a good deal at a 'bargain' price; or it can have an adverse effect if the City is concerned at the increased number of shares available, or the purposes for which the rights cash will be used.

If the shares in the rights issue are offered at a price well below the existing share price, then this is called a *deep discount* rights issue. Why offer new shares at, say, 50p when the current share price of the existing shares is 95p? The reason is to make the rights issue shares appear to be an irresistible bargain so that all the shareholders will buy their rights entitlement. This saves the company from having to pay an underwriting fee to institutions and others who would have guaranteed to buy all the rights issue shares not taken up by existing shareholders.

Much less common is a rights issue where the rights shares are offered at a *higher* price than the quoted price of the existing shares on the date the offer was first announced.

Such an offer might be made in the hope that it will appear less attractive to shareholders. Perhaps the rights issue is being underwritten by an existing shareholder, or by a person or company that hopes the issue will not be fully subscribed so that it can take up all the shares not taken up by the other shareholders. This might then enable the underwriter to acquire a large enough shareholding in the company to be able to 'influence' it into activities that will justify that higher price (and more) so that a profit can ultimately be made on the investment, and/or the company can be built into a larger one. Or perhaps the high rights price is simply due to the directors feeling that the pre-rights price of the company's shares significantly under-valued the net worth of the company and its prospects. The high rights price will highlight the directors' views (particularly if they are also shareholders in the company and will be taking up their rights entitlement) that the company deserves a better Stock Market rating.

Sometimes, instead of offering ordinary shares in a rights issue, shareholders are offered convertible loan stock which, at certain times, can be converted into shares in the company. Or they might be offered a mixture of loan stock and shares, or warrants and shares.

Taking up a rights entitlement enables an investor to add to his shareholding in a company without having to pay a stockbroker's buying commission.

What To Look For In A Rights Issue

When a rights issue is announced it is important to see how the market reacts to the news. Quite often, the announcement will produce an immediate fall in the quoted price of the company's existing shares.

This fall may be partly due to a reaction to supply-and-demand; if a company has 500 million shares in issue and announces a rights issue of a further 100 million shares, then clearly there will be many more shares in issue and perhaps there will be insufficient people and institutions wanting to acquire those shares at a fairly high price and hold on to them: the price therefore falls.

What does the company propose to do with the money raised from the rights issue? Does it plan a take-over bid (in which case, sometimes it might be more profitable to buy shares in its potential bid targets)? Does it plan to expand its existing business?

Will the money raised be used to repay some of the company's high-interest debt?

If the company has sound, sensible reasons for having a rights issue that will add to the quality and profits of the business, then it might prove attractive.

Will the directors of the company be taking up their rights entitlement? Are major institutional shareholders in the company likely to take up their rights? If not, does this imply that they lack a certain amount of confidence in the immediate future prospects of the company?

Many rights issues are accompanied by profits forecasts: do they show sound, future growth, or do they demonstrate a 'plodding' progress or even a downturn in results?

Before taking up rights issue shares, consider if your money could be better employed elsewhere. If you buy the shares, will you need to sell them shortly after purchase because you need the money for another purpose? If so, consider what price the shares might be at the time of your possible sale: is a profit still likely?

Also ask yourself: if the current share price was the same as the rights issue price, but the company was *not* having a rights issue, would you buy more shares in the company? If the answer is 'no', then look for extra reasons (if any) why the rights issue should give the company increased investment appeal to you.

I am particularly attracted to rights issues at a good discount to the current share price from small companies that are seeking extra funds to acquire another company (hopefully at a 'bargain price') or to expand in some other way the existing business: *and* the directors and any very large shareholders are committed to taking up their rights.

Timing Matters

The details of a rights issue will include a timetable of expected events, which should include the date when provisional allotment letters for the rights issue shares will be despatched (these set out how many shares each shareholder can subscribe for and how much they will cost). The timetable will also give the latest date for acceptance of the rights offer and where payment has to be made.

It is usually best *not* to pay the required sum the minute the allotment letter arrives. Perhaps the market generally will nose-dive, or comments in the press about some aspect of the company concerned might cause its shares to fall below the rights issue price.

So long as you bear in mind possible postal delays, etc., it frequently pays to delay a decision on whether or not to accept the offer until it is more clear as to what is likely to happen to the share price of the company. Also, if you send off a cheque early you will be losing the interest which you could have earned on your money.

There is little point in accepting an offer for rights issue shares if, before the first day of dealings in those shares, the quoted price of the other shares in the company has fallen well below the rights offer price, or there are other circumstances which you feel might depress the company's share price.

Remember, you are *not* obliged to take up your rights issue entitlement.

Sometimes, it is possible to raise a useful sum by selling

your rights in the market: ask your broker about the possibilities when the allotment letter arrives.

On some occasions, the announcement of a rights issue is an indication that not only should an investor *not* take up his rights entitlement, but that he should sell all or some of his existing shares in the company concerned.

Such action might be taken if the company is using the money raised from the issue to pay what the investor considers to be a very steep price for another company, and/or he feels that many of the company's shareholders will not be firm holders of the shares, even if they do take up their rights entitlement. This could mean that there might be a steady stream of sellers of the shares which could depress the share price for several months, or perhaps even for a year or more. A prompt sale could thus enable an investor to 'rescue' his money so that it can be used for a more attractive investment.

Many rights issues are attractive – some are extremely *unattractive*: so think carefully before you accept your rights – they may not be a right worth having.

Rights issues can also provide an indication as to the possible future state of the Stock Market as a whole. When there is a sudden flood of rights issues, consider if this is due to a pent-up demand for extra cash that has only just been released – or is it that some company directors feel that if their company does not raise extra funds now, it may soon be too late for them to do so? Are they expecting a general downturn in the market – or more difficult trading conditions that would make it much less easy to have a rights issue later in the year, or perhaps the following year?

If there is a rush of rights issues, will there be a considerable increase in take-over activity with the proceeds of the rights issues largely going to fund such take-overs? If so, will this help to buoy the market with an ever-increasing number of take-overs and rumours of take-overs?

What do newspaper columnists – and your stockbroker – say about these matters? What is your own 'gut reaction' to the rights issue rush?

Chapter 8:

Investing Overseas

Foreign Experience And Opportunities

Investing overseas can be profitable as well as complicated. It can also prove far more costly than investing in UK shares as dealing charges may well be higher, your dividends from foreign companies might be subjected to 'withholding tax' (a tax deducted by the country where the company concerned is based), and the cost of banking small foreign currency dividend cheques can sometimes almost 'wipe out' the entire value of the cheque. You also have to be careful that foreign exchange rate changes do not turn your profits into losses. The cost of following the progress of your shares can be quite high if you have to subscribe to foreign publications and specialist websites.

However, the profits to be made from overseas shares (if you know what you are doing) can be considerable, both from buying shares in companies that are world famous and/or have undervalued assets, and from investing in a few much more risky small companies involved in very speculative ventures.

Years ago I bought shares in a small Canadian mining company quoted in Vancouver at around 45 cents per share. Not much has since matched the exhilaration of seeing the share price soar to over Can.$8, selling the shares, watching them rise a bit more and then plummet almost as

138

steeply as their original rise. Risky: yes – the main problem being that you *must* be able to monitor the market and keep track of the progress of your shares – which can be rather difficult if you can only speak English and you buy shares in small Japanese companies which may never receive a direct mention in UK or US newspapers, and whose reports to shareholders are entirely in Japanese!

It is therefore easier to invest in companies that are covered by readily available publications and on websites in a language you understand – although this could well include subscribing to specialist websites and to airmail editions of appropriate foreign publications. Many stock-brokers can also provide advice and research material on some of the major overseas companies.

Personal experience also pays. If you go abroad on a business trip or a holiday, buy the local newspapers, ask people their opinion as to which companies they think are well-managed, and look around you.

The first time I went on holiday in Hawaii I was struck by the many thousands of Japanese tourists and by the number of Japanese at that time who were buying property and other assets in Hawaii at seemingly ever-increasing prices.

I bought shares in a US company engaged in 'diversified industries' for US$24.88 because although the company had reported losses, it owned over 50,000 acres of Hawaii. I hoped that either the company would be 'turned around' – possibly with some of its land sold at high prices – or perhaps the company would be taken over.

I was easily able to follow the company's progress as it was one of the US companies whose share price was quoted in the *Financial Times* every day.

Two years after my purchase of some of the company's shares, a Chicago-based property company made a take-over offer of US$49 per share for it.

I have also made useful profits from shares in other foreign companies – my interest in them initially being triggered by a visit to the countries in which they are based and/or by reading reports of their progress, using their products and generally keeping an eye open for suitable buying opportunities.

Do You Need An Overseas Broker?

The answer is: No. A UK broker should be able to buy shares for you overseas. You are probably much safer dealing with a broker in the UK – at least he will speak English, and phone calls, etc., will be cheaper and communications should be quicker and easier than if you have to contact a broker overseas yourself.

Your UK broker will probably have to deal for you via one of his firm's overseas subsidiaries or associates, or with a completely separate firm.

However, not all UK brokers are willing to handle dealings in certain foreign countries, so you may have to 'shop around' for another broker for these deals. You could ask your current broker to recommend another firm for your overseas deals, while keeping your deals in UK shares with your existing broker.

A broker will almost certainly have a 'minimum limit' per overseas deal: you will have to invest at least a certain specified amount. This is likely to be higher than the minimum level for buying UK shares.

If you plan to be a frequent 'small' investor in overseas shares and your current broker is unwilling to deal in the amounts you have available, then consider whether or not you should really be buying shares in foreign companies. Are the sums you have available to invest so small that any profits will be eaten up with brokers' commissions and other costs? Also 'shop around' for another stockbroking firm to see if their minimum levels of dealing (and costs) are the same.

Do *not* expect to pay just your 'normal' stockbroker's commission/fees: buying overseas shares is subject to the conditions prevailing in the countries concerned (which may involve higher costs) and it would also be reasonable to expect your broker to charge a higher fee/commission for the complexities of buying or selling overseas shares.

Sometimes it is impossible to buy shares in certain overseas companies – either the shares are simply not obtainable in the quantity that you require, or the dealers in the country concerned will not deal with your broker, perhaps because your order is too small. If this is the case, then choose another company – perhaps in another country – in which to invest.

Beware Of Currency Changes

Fluctuating currency rates can seriously damage your wealth.

Suppose a Japanese bought shares in a US company for US$10 each and sold those shares for US$15 each – how much profit did he make per share? The answer might be nil – or even a *loss*. It depends when the deals were done. When the Japanese first bought the shares there might have been many more yen per US dollar than when he sold them. Thus, when his sales proceeds were converted from dollars into yen he received fewer yen than he had paid out originally.

The same thing might happen to a UK investor buying US shares, or vice versa. Over the years (and sometimes, just within weeks or days) currencies can fluctuate to such an extent that profits in one currency can turn into losses in another.

This is why it is vitally important when investing in foreign shares to keep track of changes in the exchange rate and to follow newspaper reports about changing economic conditions, inflationary factors, trade deficits, and anything else that might affect the exchange rate of a foreign country with that of your own.

Beware Of Being A 'Foreigner'

Some countries place various restrictions on overseas investors. For example, in certain countries registered shares can only be bought by locals – foreigners have to buy, instead, the companies' 'bearer shares' or 'participation certificates' which have no voting rights.

In a number of countries, foreign investment is only allowed up to a specified limit in some television stations; and many countries limit the amount of investment foreigners can make in certain 'defence industries' such as companies manufacturing highly sophisticated weapons systems.

Before buying shares in foreign companies it is wise to ask your stockbroker if there are any limits on the amount of foreign investment that can be made in the company in which you propose to invest. If there are such limits, then ask him if he knows if those limits have already or nearly been reached.

You do not want to pay out money for shares which, perhaps a week or a month or so later, you are told you cannot take up because you are a foreigner; and nor do you want to acquire shares in a company which perhaps finds that foreigners are in breach of the limits and so, on a 'last one in, first one out' basis you are forced to sell your shares – perhaps at a depressed price.

Some countries insist that share certificates of their companies must remain in their country. This means you will probably have to pay extra for a broker or bank to 'hold' your share certificate in the country concerned or perhaps your shares might be registered in a 'marking name' instead of in your own name.

A 'marking name' might be an overseas bank or stockbroker holding the shares on your behalf. The problem with a 'marking name' is that the 'name' usually receives the company reports, circulars, etc. The investor will probably have to request specifically that these documents are sent on to him and, even then, there can sometimes be delays in forwarding the company reports, circulars, etc to the investor.

Countries that are likely to fall on 'very hard times' might introduce foreign exchange restrictions which could mean that, if you sold shares in companies in that country, you might not be able to get all your money out of that country.

Foreigners are sometimes regarded as 'easy prey' by overseas confidence tricksters. They might discover your name from a foreign company share register and contact you to suggest that you invest in various highly profitable-sounding investments. Check these people out. Has your broker ever heard of them and the companies they are recommending? Do *not* risk your money with people or companies about whom you know little or nothing, no matter how 'good' the proposed deal may sound.

There are many other problems of being a 'foreigner' investing in overseas shares – including the poor postal services of some countries which means that by the time you receive company circulars regarding, say, a take-over offer, the acceptance deadline for that offer has already passed.

Check with your broker about the current problems in the country of your proposed investment before you invest.

'Board Lots' and 'Odd Lots'

Some countries expect investors to deal in 'board lots' – investors are expected to buy a minimum number (a 'board lot') of shares in a company.

Other countries expect shares to be bought in 'round lots' which are multiples of 100 (or in multiples of 10 for companies whose shares are not traded very actively).

If you buy, say, 79 shares instead of 100 you will be buying what is known as an 'odd lot' and the cost per share will work out as somewhat more than if you had bought a 'round lot'.

Therefore, before placing a firm 'buy' order with your broker, ask him if there are any 'lot' customs which might increase (or reduce) the cost of your proposed investment. You might then consider purchasing instead a more suitable 'lot'.

Settlement Systems

The settlement systems of various countries are subject to change. Some countries require shares to be paid for within five days of purchase, others require payment within one or two days, and others have still different settlement systems. In some countries payment on share sales will only take place when a share certificate has been physically handed over to the new owner's broker.

Check with your broker before dealing as to the settlement system that will be used – do *not* simply assume that it will be the same as for buying and selling UK shares in the UK.

If you are buying overseas shares in the hope of making some short-term gains then, before you buy, ask your stockbroker if he knows roughly how long it might take for a share certificate in the company concerned actually to be delivered by the company's registration agents.

It has been known for people to buy shares in certain overseas companies for a very modest amount and then see the price of the shares more than double within six months. Unfortunately, they are then unable to sell the shares and take a profit as they are still waiting for their share certificates to arrive and, without possession of the share certificates, the rule of that country's Stock Market means that they are unable to sell the shares. The shares then plunge in value so that by the time the share certificates arrive (more than six months after the shares were purchased) the investors can only sell the shares at a great loss.

What To Do With Foreign Dividends

Many countries deduct tax from dividend payments. To avoid being taxed overseas *and* in the UK on the *same* dividend (paying tax twice) check with your broker or financial adviser as to whether or not there is a double taxation treaty with the country in which you have investments. If there is such a treaty, then you can hopefully mitigate some of your tax.

Some banks make a 'minimum charge' for clearing foreign cheques and if you receive a small foreign currency dividend cheque this charge might take away a large portion of that dividend. To avoid this, you might be able to open a bank account in the country concerned and arrange for the dividends to be paid into that account until they have built up into a sufficient sum to make a repatriation of funds to the UK worthwhile; or the accumulated dividends might be sufficient to allow further purchases of shares in companies in that country. You could also consider visiting that country for a holiday and using those dividends as an addition to your spending money. Of course, you will still have to pay any tax that might be due on those dividends.

Multi-Nationals And Other Companies

The investor looking for a suitable overseas share to buy might decide to look for a company whose name he has at least heard of and which also does business in many other countries as well as the one in which it has its main headquarters. This makes finding out about their new products much easier as you may well be buying them yourself!

One of the advantages of buying shares in multi-nationals is that a number of them are quoted not only on the stock markets of their 'home' country, but also on the London Stock Market and on Wall Street: this makes it somewhat easier to buy their shares.

While some multi-nationals produce excellent returns for their investors, there will always be much less well known and more 'local' companies in each country whose share performance might surpass that of the multi-national. The problem is: how do you find such companies?

The answer is: by reading newspapers and magazines; assessing 'tips' from your broker; travelling abroad; trying to understand the culture, economy and politics of various countries; close scrutiny of the reports and actions of various companies; and trying to discover what helps to make certain stock markets rise and fall.

Do not ignore the possibility of investing in a multi-national company – many of them have excellent management – but also consider the possibility of investing in a smaller or less well-known foreign company.

Remember that investment in a foreign company may be risky: only invest money you can afford to lose.

Selected World Stock Markets

What follows are some personal, brief, observations on stock markets in a number of different countries.

It is not possible in a book of this size to go into great detail, or to recommend any individual shares as conditions are always changing, but I have tried to mention a few of the factors that can influence the movement of some of the share prices in those countries. My comments represent my own feelings – and some people may not agree with them.

There are many other stock markets around the world apart from those outlined on the following pages. For example in: Austria, Belgium, Brazil, Denmark, Finland, Mexico, New Zealand, Norway, Philippines, Sweden, Thailand and Turkey.

Use your own judgment, instincts, and the knowledge and experience of yourself and your broker to choose the countries (and shares) most suitable for your own investment.

However, investing directly in companies in some of the 'emerging markets' can present all sorts of difficulties to the private investor. If this area of activity appeals to you then, rather than investing directly, consider the investment possibilities of unit trusts and/or investment trusts specialising in those areas.

Australia

Lots of fun can be had with Australian shares – especially in small companies involved in mining: their share prices can soar on rumours of a new gold or other metal find – and then plummet just as rapidly if the rumours prove to be unfounded.

Close monitoring of the market is therefore essential – as is a regular watch on metal prices. Even then, it will be quite difficult to beat the performance of some Australian investors who are obviously much 'closer' to various rumours, etc., than an overseas investor can hope to be.

A glut of a particular metal and a consequent slump in its world price can have dramatic effects on some Australian companies' shares. Similarly, a shortage of a particular metal can force prices to rise rapidly and this, too, might produce a rise in certain mining company shares.

Agriculture also plays a large part in Australia's economy, and if there have been poor farming conditions in Europe, Canada and the US then, if Australian conditions have been better, this should also hopefully be reflected in the share prices of companies with large agricultural interests.

The Australian Stock Market is also particularly influenced by conditions on the Wall Street and Tokyo markets. The share prices of certain large companies can also be influenced by the ease (or otherwise) of gaining and retaining large loans from US and other banks.

Canada

Toronto is the major stock exchange and companies involved in paper and forestry products, mining and other natural resources can be the subject of interesting movements in their share prices, depending on the fluctuating worldwide demand for their products.

Some of the small mining and high technology companies quoted on the Canadian Venture Exchange can sometimes have dramatic rises (and falls) in their share prices.

The Canadian Stock Markets are also influenced by trading on Wall Street. If the US Market suffers a severe set-back this can cause 'sentiment' for Canadian shares to be affected too, and thus a drop in Canadian share prices.

France

Unless you can speak and read French and understand French politics and the French character, then be very careful about investing in French companies.

Politics seems to play a more important role in the rises and falls of shares in certain French companies than it would do in some other countries.

The general French belief in their own 'uniqueness', which borders on arrogance, means that nearly all decisions will be made on the basis of what is best for France and the French – and if 'foreigners' suffer a loss on their investment then this may result in just a typical shrug of French shoulders.

Germany

The German Stock Market is one of the largest in the world, but many German companies seem to have something of a reputation for being rather unexciting.

The complex management and voting share structure of some German companies make them unlikely to be the subject of contested take-over bids, so this should be borne in mind by any investor hoping to make gains from take-over rumours: check out the share structure before you invest.

I am not particularly attracted to the German market as I don't speak or read German – but if I thought that one of Germany's chemicals or pharmaceuticals companies was about to announce a new, exciting 'discovery' which could produce dramatic gains in its share price, then I might 'gamble' a modest amount.

Japan

The Japanese Stock Market is like a pair of chopsticks: considerably more difficult for a 'foreigner' to use with ease than for a 'native'. The Japanese do everything in their own particular way, and I suspect that the market is subject to considerable 'manipulation' with Government officials 'helping' to influence market conditions by changing taxation regulations, trading rules, investment regulations, accountancy regulations, etc., in order to try to make the market reflect the level that Government officials and/or 'big business' want it to reflect.

It is worth remembering that shortly after the 'Crash of '87', the Japanese authorities decided to ease the accounting rules for *tokkin* funds. *Tokkin* are funds run by companies to deal in other companies' shares.

For example, if a Japanese chemical company thought its manufacturing profits might be hit by the high yen or a drop in demand, it might speculate aggressively on the stock market in an attempt to boost its results by means of share dealing profits. This became known as *zaitech* – or 'financial engineering'.

The '87 Crash brought problems – but the Japanese authorities allowed *tokkin* fund managers to give, in their 1987 and 1988 accounts, the value of their shareholdings at purchase cost, ignoring any losses suffered in the Crash.

Such official encouragement for 'manipulative accounting' has made me very wary of the Japanese market: you never know when it might be promoted again!

An investor may be attracted to a particular company

because of its innovative products – and then find that a large proportion of its profits has not derived from sales of those products, but from highly speculative dealings in the bond futures market!

Many Japanese companies have 'strategic shareholdings' in other Japanese companies in order to help 'business relationships'. Japanese companies generally have higher p/e ratios and give much lower dividend yields than companies in the UK, USA and many other countries.

Land and property in Japan is still highly priced compared to some other countries – yet many heavily populated areas are in earthquake-prone regions. In the event of any trouble, some bureaucrats could be slow and indecisive.

Major stockbrokers appear to have more influence than their counterparts in most other countries. If one of them strongly recommends the purchase of a particular share, then it is more likely that the share concerned might attract buying attention.

I think the Japanese market is best left to 'experts' – especially as the market seems to be run mainly for the benefit of the Japanese and, if it ever came to a real 'crunch' it is likely that non-Japanese investors would be the first to suffer.

Malaysia

Successful investment in Malaysian companies requires a sound knowledge of the current Malaysian political scene (as politics plays an extremely important role in share price levels) unless you merely want a quick speculative 'punt' in a company producing a particular commodity (such as palm oil or tin) at a time when you feel it might become in short supply.

Netherlands

Unless you are investing in a Dutch-based multi-national company where you are looking for steady growth, then pay careful attention to a firm's board structure and any anti-take-over devices it may have adopted. For some Dutch companies, it is very difficult for shareholders to remove poor management or for such companies to be taken over.

A close study of the market might prove rewarding, but it is probably better to invest hoping for long-term gains rather than expecting gains in the short term.

Singapore

The Singapore Stock Market is particularly vulnerable to what happens in Malaysia and it is also affected by 'sentiment' on Wall Street and by political decisions in Singapore. Political changes in China and Thailand can also affect the Singapore Stock Market.

The Singapore economy owes much to the country's ability to export manufactured goods, and any imposition of further restrictive export quotas on Singapore will probably affect the share prices of many of its companies.

Switzerland

Swiss companies are more focused on securing their long-term future than on short-term deals. Therefore, if investors find the Swiss market attractive, they should either invest in companies hoping for longer-term gains, or hope to make gains in the short to medium term from Swiss companies that might benefit from the discovery of a new drug or perhaps be favourably affected by adverse conditions, currency devaluations, etc., elsewhere in the world.

USA

I have had a number of successful US investments. What I look for in a US company is much the same as I would look for in a UK company: good management; excellent profits (or 'turn-round' potential); a fairly low p/e; sound assets; and, in some cases, the possibility that the company might be a take-over target.

Initially, I used the London office of a large US stockbroker – but I found the service left something to be desired and so I used my UK London broker instead.

It seems to me that many US brokers have lots of 'sales executives' and 'financial consultants' whose job appears to be to get people to buy (or sell) as much as possible so that they get more commissions and better bonuses, while their actual knowledge of many US companies may perhaps be less than your own.

For example, one 'financial consultant' asked me if I wanted any research on US companies. I named a company in which I was interested.

'That's not one of the stocks we follow,' said the consultant.

I patiently explained that the company concerned was one of the major entertainment corporations in the US.

'Oh, yes,' came the response, amidst sounds of papers being rapidly shuffled and computer keys being pressed. 'We do follow that. Shall I send you the research?'

I said 'Yes, please,' and soon afterwards received a computer print-out of about 20 lines which didn't tell me anything about the company which I hadn't already easily discovered.

A short time later I mentioned that perhaps the brokerage firm had some information on another company which I named.

This produced the response: 'Not heard of that one before – and we follow 1,500 stocks.'

Again, I patiently explained that it was another major US entertainments corporation. Again, there were sounds of shuffled papers and keys being pressed – this time followed by an astonished cry: 'Oh yes! And it's even a stock we recommend!'

When I did eventually buy some US shares via this particular firm they managed to get the shares registered to 'Kevin Grierson c/o Goldstein-Jackson' rather than in my full names of 'Kevin Grierson Goldstein-Jackson'. This meant the share certificates had to be returned to the registrar of the company concerned so that they could be replaced by correctly addressed certificates.

It was at this point that I abandoned using a US broker. However, I should hastily point out that there *are* many good US brokers who *are* knowledgeable and efficient – it was just my misfortune to have chanced upon a firm that appeared to be having some problems . . .

US brokers are so keen to get people to deal in shares that they will try to persuade some investors to buy 'on margin', only paying cash for 50 per cent of the cost of the shares, with the broker lending the investors the remainder of the money, but reserving the right to sell the shares if they fall below a certain level. This has led to some people getting in 'out of their depth' and investing far more than they could sensibly afford to lose and being severely hurt when the market has suddenly fallen sharply.

US brokers' perceptions of time appear to be very short. For example, to a US broker, 'the near term' means 'from today to five weeks'; 'medium term' means 'from five weeks to six months'; and 'long term' is defined as 'anything more than six months.'

There is a tendency amongst institutional and other investors based in the US to look for short-term gains, rather than looking towards the longer-term potential.

Great stress is placed on US companies' quarterly performances. This can inhibit some companies from investing in new, improved manufacturing capability and increasing research spending if it will have the effect of reducing quarterly earnings in the short to medium term.

Many Americans are now 'day traders'. They spend hours every day surfing the internet looking for news, tips and other information that they hope will enable them to buy shares and sell them at a profit within hours or days. Day traders will often dump shares in firms whose short-term profits disappoint.

However, a company that has been a reasonable dividend payer, but has conserved cash to fund research that may pay off in a very big way, or which has developed new manufacturing processes that will sharply reduce costs and considerably under-cut the opposition, should surely have a higher rate of share price increase in the long term than a company that pays high dividends, does not replace out-dated plant and technology and fails to develop new, improved and cheaper products. Some of the companies of the latter sort could eventually show a slump in profits and a consequent drop in share price.

The US is a very litigious nation. Before investing in a US company I always try to find out from its annual report, press comments, brokers' reports, etc., as to whether or not the company has any large outstanding legal actions against it – or is in some way involved in the sort of business (chemical waste dumping, dealing with hazardous materials, etc.) that might possibly turn out one year to have serious financial consequences if anything went wrong.

I also try to avoid companies that are heavily in debt (or 'mortgaged up to their eyeballs'), and companies that have loaned large sums to people, companies or countries that may be unwilling or unable to repay those loans on properly commercial terms.

There are also a number of US companies with poor management. Sometimes, the managers of poorly performing large US companies have enormous salaries and considerable benefits (including private planes) but the managers own few shares in their companies. I would not invest in such corporations unless I thought another company or 'corporate raider' might take-over the company and 'sort it out', including removing the poor management.

I prefer to invest in companies where the management has a vested interest in its success – such as a reasonably large shareholding or a bonus scheme based on improvements to the company's profit performance to shareholders – and judged not just on short-term gains. I also like companies that have undervalued assets.

The US market as a whole seems much more susceptible to reactions due to 'sentiment' than some other markets. Perhaps this is due to the fact that a large part of all personal wealth in the US is invested in the equity markets – a much higher proportion than in most other countries. The Americans therefore tend to have a greater interest in the progress of the Stock Market (and greater fears for its future state) because what happens to the market might well seriously affect their personal wealth.

Thus, the US market is one in which it pays to have some local knowledge and some understanding of how many investors might react to certain political events, economic circumstances, etc.

Chapter 9:

How To Make Money In A Stock Market Slump

The easiest way to make money in a Stock Market slump is to anticipate its arrival and sell all (or most) of your shares before the slump (or Crash) happens.

However, few people (myself included) can bear to part with *every* share they own, even if they believe very strongly that a Crash is about to happen. Why? For two main reasons:

1. Although they believe a Crash is on its way, in the back of their mind is the lingering thought that maybe they are wrong: what happens if they sell absolutely everything – even the shares in a company that looks as if it is ripe for a take-over – and the Crash doesn't happen? The take-over target then gets a bid that makes its share price more than double in one month! The thought of such an event can easily deter a share sale.

2. Some of the shares in an investor's portfolio might be in very small companies where the market in them is very 'tight' – there are few sellers of the shares. Perhaps the company is family-controlled. Perhaps there is a very patient investor who believes that one day he might be able to take-over the company: every time some shares come on the

157

market, he buys them – even during a Crash.

Therefore, if an investor sells his shares in such a company, he may find it very difficult (or even impossible) to buy them back again, and thus he will miss out on any long-term gains which might be considerable.

Shares which do *not* fall into either of these categories should be sold if a Crash looks imminent. Even shares with 'take-over' hopes should be sold if they have not got sound, solid assets that are worth considerably more than their share price.

However, the liquidation of a share portfolio may well also have considerable tax implications and so some investors might be reluctant to sell too many of their shareholdings, perhaps because it might give rise to a large tax bill. They might also fear that if their 'reading' of the Market turns out to be wrong, and a Crash does not happen, and share prices continue to move upwards, then they would have less money (as a result of paying tax on their share sales) with which to 'buy back' into the Market. It is therefore helpful to ask your financial adviser to assess what your likely tax liabilities would be if you sold all (or most) of your shares, and then carefully consider whether or not tax considerations outweigh the benefits to be gained from not having to see all your shares plummet dramatically in price in the event of a Crash.

An investor should be prepared to see *all* his shares suffer in a Crash – even those with strong asset-backing.

Faced with a Crash, there is no time for loyalty to a particular share. Even shares in companies with excellent track records, future growth potential, etc., should be sold because, unfortunately, 'quality' shares are marked down in price in a Crash, along with the 'junk'. They may not fall as much, but they will still be marked down in price.

It is important to remember that while many share prices

will fall in a Crash due to the numbers of shares being sold, some share prices will be marked down in price by the market makers, even if few (if any) deals have been done in those shares. The market makers are simply trying to protect their position: they don't want to take on to their books shares which they think might be difficult to 'unload': a sharply reduced price helps to deter people from offering the shares for sale in the first place!

Crash Warnings

How does a person know when a Crash is imminent? It would be nice to be able to say that I accurately predicted the Crash of '87 due to careful research, computerized studies of Stock Market trends, etc: something 'concrete' that could be used to indicate any future major falls in the Market.

Unfortunately, my accuracy was due to a 'hunch', a 'feeling' that the Market was due to fall sharply. I am not one of the people who 'predicted' a crash every year for five or ten years before it actually happened!

I first commented on the possibility of a slump in the Market in an article in the *Financial Times* on 18th April 1987, when I pointed out that the year 'might prove somewhat similar to 1973-74' and so I had sold some of my shares 'just in case there is a sudden and prolonged downturn in the market.'

I was soon tempted back into the Market by ever-rising share prices. However, by August 1987 I was convinced a Crash was on its way. My article in the *Financial Times* of 1st August was headed 'Fear Of The Crash'.

Share prices around the world had risen to incredible heights. The average p/e of US companies was at its highest level for 26 years. Movements on the London Stock Market seemed increasingly to be influenced by rumours, trade figures, Wall Street, and amorphous 'sentiment' – all of which indicated to me that a number of the City's 'professional players' were nervous.

I noticed all this as an 'outsider'. My articles for the *Financial Times* were based on my own personal experiences as a private investor – I was not a professional financial journalist. Nor was I working in the City, or for a broker or banker at the time. Instead, I gained my 'impressions' from small items in newspapers, and generally just watching share price movements and looking at company news.

I was concerned about the US fund managers who engaged in 'computer trading'. Computers were programmed so that if the Market fell generally, or in a particular sector, by a pre-set amount, then the computers would automatically issue orders to sell certain shares. Similarly, if the market rose by a pre-set amount, certain shares would be purchased. There were all sorts of computer variations on this.

I was concerned about the growing 'indexation' of funds where increasing numbers of financial institutions invested mainly in shares that made up Standard and Poor's 500 share index or even the FT-SE 100 index. If the Stock Market dropped dramatically, fund managers could still produce a chart showing that their funds had not underperformed an 'index' – because their funds were only invested in the shares that made up that index.

I was concerned, too, by financial institutions playing 'pass the parcel' with shares. As mentioned earlier in this book, certain fund managers bought shares on Monday, sold them to another institution a day or so later at a slightly higher price, that institution in turn sold them to another a few days later, and so on.

Turnover on world stock markets had shot up, largely

because of institutions playing 'pass the parcel' – but what would happen if no one wanted to keep the parcel when the music stopped?

I thought I also detected increasing signs of arrogance amongst some of the 'professionals' – the analysts, fund managers, etc. – who pontificated in print and on TV about the state of the Market. They were making lots of money in the City. The Market was booming. They were super-confident in their own ability, that what they said was right: if they said share prices would keep rising, then that is what shares would do.

It often seems to me that when people appear arrogant they are either 'blustering', hoping to hide some fear that perhaps not all is well – or perhaps they are rather stupid, convinced that they can do no wrong. *Everyone* makes mistakes. Not everyone *admits* to making them. I therefore had a feeling (perhaps even a hope) that the arrogant know-alls were heading for a fall!

In my August article I commented that perhaps the shares of companies in various 'indices' were higher than perhaps they might otherwise be – simply due to the over-attention such shares had been given by the indexed funds. What would happen if they got 'hit' by the 'computer' traders?

The problem with many fund managers (as I mentioned earlier in this book) is that they tend to 'follow the herd'. Perhaps some of them also felt that the Market was too high, but were afraid of selling too many of their share-holdings in case they were wrong and their funds ended up being under-invested and thus under-performed the funds of their rivals. Fear of 'getting it wrong' perhaps made some of them 'hold on' for too long.

Of course, when some major institutions started selling and the 'panic' spread, most of the fund managers rushed to 'get out' of as many shares as possible.

By early October of 1987 I felt convinced that a Crash was about to happen, and in my *Financial Times* article, published on 17th October (but written almost a week earlier) I pointed out that in July I had started to sell my unit trust holdings and some shares, and in September had reduced my shareholdings considerably.

I wrote: 'I sense that stock markets around the world – particularly Wall Street – are very nervous and further sharp declines could well occur.'

On 19th October, the Dow Jones share index in New York fell by 508 points, and in London the FT-SE 100 Index fell by 250 points!

One of the other factors that pointed the way to a Crash was the great leap in share prices in 1986/87 of companies that were simply not worth the money. Many share prices were completely mad.

I had observed a few companies report horrendous results (even losses), only to see their share prices rise dramatically on the announcement of their figures. Even if people had rushed to buy the shares on take-over hopes, at least one of the companies concerned had so few assets (and was in such bad financial shape) that it was extremely unlikely to be taken over at the then current highly inflated share price, or even at a fifty per cent discount to that price!

After the Crash, a lot of 'professionals' said: 'Of course, the Market was a bubble waiting to burst.' How many of them said that *before* the Crash – or took proper 'evasive action'?

So, if you have a 'hunch' or 'feeling' that a Crash is about to happen – why not follow your feelings and substantially reduce your share portfolio? You could be right, and the 'professionals' might be wrong!

Beware Of A Creeping Crash

If a stock market plunges 500 points in a day, investors take notice and worry. But if it drops by, say, 100 points one day, rises by 50 points the next, then falls 200 points, then rises by 95 points, people might overlook that the average trend is sharply downwards and might be a signal that share prices have reached unsustainable levels. If the pattern continues for months and an investor has retained all his shares, his losses from this 'creeping crash' could be far greater than if the market had crashed 500 points in a day.

Crash Action

Assuming you act in time and have sold shares before a Crash, what do you do with all the cash during the slump? What actions you take depend on what sort of an investor you are.

If you are naturally cautious, then keep most of the cash in a bank that you know is sound, or consider putting some of that cash into either a foreign bank or into a foreign currency account of a British bank. Choose a country/ currency that you or your advisers feel will be stable during a slump, and a currency that should perform well against the £ and US$. Hopefully, not only will you get interest on your money, but will benefit from foreign exchange rate changes during the slump.

Some advisers might recommend (as well as cash in the bank) a modest investment in gold, platinum, or some other precious metal. Whether or not this is worthwhile will depend on the economic circumstances at the time, the price of the metals concerned, the likely future demand for those metals, and the ease and speed with which they can be sold.

Investors who like taking risks can survey the state of a shattered Stock Market and look for shares that have been marked down perhaps too heavily, and might buy them in the hope that the share price will perk up again and they can take a quick profit. This is a gamble.

Investors who are seeking long-term gains can wait a while after the first few awful days of a Crash and see if the Market has further to fall. Perhaps some institutions will continue their 'rush for cash', if only to show in their year-end accounts that they had a higher percentage of assets in cash than at the end of the previous year, thus hoping that an investor might think the institution had accumulated that cash pile *before* the Crash (having antici-pated its arrival) rather than *after* it. This sort of action can help to keep prices depressed.

If it looks as if the continued fall in the Market might be 'gentle', or if the Market just appears lack-lustre and slug-gish, then investors can search for shares in companies with very strong asset-backing (worth considerably more than the share price) and buy some of those shares.

The price might well fall still further, but they can hope that within, say, 3 to 5 years, the share price will have risen to new heights. This requires patience and really should only appeal to investors who do not mind having their money 'tied up' for some time and who will not need it urgently for other purposes.

However, if a Crash turns into a Depression, then prop-erty prices can fall heavily; and even companies that used to find their products in popular demand might find that their sales have plunged.

Some investors might also look for shares offering high dividend yields – so long as they are reasonably confident that the companies concerned are well run and unlikely to have to cut their dividends.

Some investors may consider a combination of all these tactics.

Remember: you do *not* have to invest. If you have any serious worries about the state of the Market then: when in doubt, keep out!

Chapter 10:

What *Really* Decides A Share Price?

Earlier in this book, we have seen that there are all sorts of factors that can help to decide whether or not a share price goes up or down: does a company have good management? – good products? – excellent future prospects? Is it a take-over target? Does it have undervalued assets? Are the costs of its raw materials going up? Is the company going to be affected by new laws, perhaps banning or restricting the sales of some of its products, or imposing higher taxes on them? Have the shares been recommended as a 'buy' or 'sell' by share tipsters?

However, while all the above things may *help* to decide a share price, what *really* and *finally* decides it, is the price that someone is prepared to pay for the share. This may seem a simple statement, but it took me several years to believe it.

Personal Experience

When I first started investing, I used to think that a share price was *entirely* based on the value of a company's assets, the quality of its management, the quality and popularity of its products, its future prospects, and so on.

Yet sometimes I would buy shares where the assets per share were worth much more than the share price. The

166

share price remained unmoved – or moved only slightly.

I would carefully research p/e ratios and buy shares in a company with good prospects which had a p/e less than most of the other companies in its sector. Nothing much happened to the share price.

I would carefully study the market in the engineering sector and buy shares in a few companies that were doing very well. For some of them, their share prices went up – for others, the share prices went down.

I initially avoided investing in one particular company whose shares I thought were over-priced, as the company concerned had a number of problems. Its share price went up still further, and some people were 'tipping' it to go higher still. I bought some of the shares, although I remained convinced that the shares were over-valued. The share price went even higher. I sold most of my shares in it at a good profit. The share price continued up and up: investors seemed to *love* the shares. Then the company went into liquidation and a lot of people lost a lot of money.

'Correct' Prices

Look at the shares of certain manufacturing companies before and after the 'Crash of '87'. What was the 'correct' price of their shares? The businesses were mostly unchanged after the Crash. They still made the same products, and people still bought those products in much the same numbers as they had before the Crash. So why did their share prices change so dramatically? Nothing else about the companies had changed: the management was the same, the products were the same, the future prospects for many were the same.

The difference in those companies before and after the Crash was that before the Crash people were prepared to pay ever greater amounts of money for their shares, whereas during and after the Crash people either did not want shares in those companies at all, or were only prepared to pay much less for those shares.

Thus a share is only worth what someone is prepared to pay for it. A share does not have some independent, guaranteed value of its own, regardless of the views of investors.

If a company in the UK, making the same sort of product as a company in Japan, and with much the same future prospects, has a share price which produces a low p/e, and the Japanese company has a p/e considerably higher: is the British company under-valued and the Japanese company over-valued – or are *both* companies wrongly rated?

And what is the 'correct' rating of a company in the US, also making similar products and with similar future prospects – if that company has a p/e level mid-way between that of the UK and Japanese companies?

If you view such p/e ratios as being based on investors' preparedness to buy shares in the companies concerned at the prices reflected in those p/es, then the share prices for each company are correct.

Too many people believe that shares have some sort of mystique – that shares are somehow 'different' from anything else that can be bought and sold. But there should be no mystique over buying and selling shares.

A share is worth whatever someone will pay for it. I make no apologies for repeating this statement. A share does *not* create an independent worth of its own any more than a house or an apple. If no one wants to buy the house or the apple, then what is it worth?

If a house or an apple does not attract a buyer, the sellers will probably eventually reduce the price of it in the hope of attracting one. They may still not find a buyer and may then decide (or be forced) to keep the house/apple.

The same is true of shares. What moves a share price is people's perceptions of where they think that share price should be. If enough people do not share your view of a share's 'worth', then the share price may not move in the way you want it to. The same applies to 'sentiment' regarding the market as a whole.

Economic Statistics

But surely economic conditions affect share prices, too? What about unemployment figures, balance of trade figures, exchange rate changes, etc? Of course, *all* of these *can* have great effects on share price levels – but look how some people 'interpret' the figures: some of the 'interpretation' is due to 'sentiment'.

For example, 'trade figures' in the UK are notorious for being the subject of 're-adjustments', 'special circumstances', and so on. If the UK's imports are far greater than its exports, but 'experts' and people in the City are generally 'happy', then they may say: 'I know the trade figures are bad – but look at the *content* of the import figures – a lot of it is machinery so that our factories can re-equip and thus increase productivity and expand our exports'; or they may say: 'The figures look awful, but you have to take a longer term view than just a few months. We are looking for improvements in the future'. Share prices may not be 'marked down' at all.

If market makers are feeling generally 'unhappy' or 'depressed' they will tend to 'forget' about the content of the trade figures (or any possible real long-term trends) and may just mark prices down sharply on their announcement, while commenting that the figures are 'disastrous'.

It is even possible for 'good news' to be viewed as 'bad'. For example, if the unemployment rate *increases*, some people may comment that it 'signals a recession'. However, if the unemployment rate *falls*, the same people might say 'the economy is in danger of overheating' – presumably because they regard anything approaching 'full employment' as being a trigger for increased wage demands, increased consumer spending, and so on.

If retail sales figures are up, they may say that this is bad because it 'fuels inflation'; if retail sales figures are down, they may say 'the consumer boom is over, people are tightening their belts, there is a downturn in the economy'.

If the US$ falls against the £, people may say 'this is terrible for UK exporters – the £ is too high. It means our goods will cost more in the States'. If people feel generally 'happy' they may say: 'What matters more is the rate of the £ against the Japanese yen and other currencies: exports should be relatively unaffected and at least imports of raw materials from the US will now be cheaper'. Or they might point out that if quality goods, and goods that people are keen to buy, are exported, they will still buy them, even if they do have to pay a bit more for them. Or they may point out how the share prices of Japanese companies still boomed between, say, 1985 and 1988, despite a hefty rise in the value of the yen against the US$.

On Wall Street one sometimes wonders if the influences of drugs, greed and fear have more effect on share prices (by their effects on the 'sentiment' of some of the people concerned) than certain economic statistics!

This is not to say that *all* economic statistics will have no effect regardless of 'sentiment'. 'Money supply figures' (basically the amount of money in circulation) can still be a pointer to changes in the inflation rate and various other economic consequences – all of which would really need another book in which to describe them and their effects properly.

Although the figures and the facts will catch up with you eventually – the actual timing of their effect will owe a lot to 'sentiment'. If politicians and people in the City are generally happy and confident, then they can 'absorb' bad news without it having too much effect on the Stock Market. If they are 'uncertain' or even 'fearful' – then watch out!

Changing Sentiment

Can people's views on particular shares and on 'sentiment' be changed?

Suppose you have bought shares in a company, believing it to be an ideal take-over target. Nothing happens. No bid approaches are made.

So why not write to the Chairman or Chief Executive of a suitable 'predator', pointing out the benefits their organization might gain if they took over the company concerned? The worst that could happen is that they will ignore your letter or write back saying 'No thanks'. On the other hand, they might actually have 'overlooked' the company and be grateful to you for drawing it to their attention and they may decide to launch a bid for it.

Suppose you hold shares in a company that is doing very well and has bright prospects, but this is not reflected in its share price. Write to the Chief Executive of the company concerned, asking him to try to publicize the company's successes better, perhaps even suggesting that the company hires a new PR firm.

Write to an appropriate financial journalist (one who 'tips' shares) on a national newspaper or financial website. Ask if he/she knows why the shares have not performed, despite the excellence of the company. The journalist may well be prevented, for legal and other reasons, from giving an individual, detailed reply – but your letter might encourage him/her to 'tip' the shares if your letter has managed to convince him/her with sound, sensible reasons that the shares should be re-rated upwards.

Maybe you can persuade your own broker of the investment merits of the company concerned, so that he will recommend it to some of his clients.

Sometimes I believe that certain people travelling in the first class sections of trains and planes try to talk up a share price. Perhaps they are travelling with a friend or business colleague and will talk in a loud voice about the merits of a particular share which they happen to own. Maybe they hope that one or two of their fellow travellers might be stockbrokers, bankers or other financial/Stock Market people and that the loud 'talking up' might persuade them to invest their money (or that of their clients) in the company or companies so loudly talked about and which they cannot help but 'overhear'.

I have occasionally 'suffered' such loud-mouthed people myself – usually while trying to have a short sleep on a train. However, such comments (like some appearing on financial website bulletin boards) may not be completely accurate.

As regards 'sentiment' to the market as a whole, unfortunately a lone individual (unless he is a country's President, Prime Minister or Chancellor of the Exchequer) is unlikely to be able dramatically and rapidly to change mass 'sentiment' – even if that 'sentiment' appears to be based on completely irrational hopes or fears.

Chapter 11:

What Do They *Really* Mean?

One of the main reasons why stockbrokers employ analysts is because they hope that analysts' comments will help persuade people to buy or sell shares and thus create more commissions and more income for the stockbrokers. It is therefore not in the nature of many analysts to say bluntly: 'There's nothing worth buying or selling. Don't bother dealing at all. Wait until an attractive opportunity arises and/or the market starts to pick up.'

Similarly, few company chairmen will admit that they and/or their management teams have made a mistake: they don't want to lose the confidence of their shareholders.

Personally, I would be very attracted to buy shares in a company where the Chairman said: 'We made a few blunders last year. We've learnt from our mistakes and have taken salary cuts as 'punishment'. We'll do better this year, I promise.' Surely this is preferable to a Chairman who makes feeble excuses and puts the blame for a poor performance on everyone and anything except himself and the 'top' management?

Having now finished all the 'serious' chapters of this book (apart from *Twenty-One Brief Basic Reminders* which follows) here is a lighthearted – but rather cynical – view of what a *few* analysts and company chairmen might mean when they use certain expressions. I stress the word '*few*':

most analysts and company chairmen (even if they use some of the expressions quoted in this chapter) do *not* play such verbal games – they really do mean what they say and should *not* have their expressions cynically re-interpreted.

Analysts

'buy' = hopefully you won't lose too much money if you buy.

'buy them for their yield'/'good for income seekers' = the share price is unlikely to rise very much, but the shares provide a reasonable dividend income.

'a good buy' = would we ever recommend a bad buy?

'good buying opportunities for sophisticated investors' = the share price will go up and then plummet – when it will plummet, we don't know, so you'll have to be smart to get out at the right time.

'a long-term buy' = the share price might well go down. If it does, don't moan to me as the shares should hopefully go up in six months or, failing that, some time within the next one to five years/we originally recommended those shares as a short-term buy, but we were wrong – now something might happen in the long term.

'look to buy' = the shares are going to fall. Hopefully, when they start to fall you'll buy some and help keep the price up.

'buy for recovery' = we tipped the shares earlier, but they went down. Hopefully, the shares will now recover if we can encourage more people to buy them.

'a quality buy' = shares in a boring, large company that is going nowhere and the shares are being bought by institutional investors but by few other people.

'the charts indicate a buy/sell' = the *charts* indicate that – but what do *people* think?

'hold' = we think the shares might go down, but we don't want to say 'sell' as we are brokers to the company concerned and they won't be very pleased if we said 'sell'.

'weak hold' = we think the shares are likely to go down, but we don't want to say 'sell' in case we are wrong.

'investors who bought at earlier prices should consider averaging down' = investors who bought at the ridiculously inflated prices at which we earlier recommended the shares, and who are now showing big losses as a result of the price collapse, should buy more of the shares at their current low prices. We hope that this extra buying will make the share price perk up a bit so that your overall loss won't look quite so bad.

'look to sell' = the shares are going to go up and you should sell them when they've gone up a bit. We might then decide to take the shares on our books and try to interest one of our major clients in making a take-over bid for the company at a very good price.

'bid rumours are in the price for nothing' = there may or may not be a take-over bid/there aren't any bid rumours apart from me saying 'bid rumours are in the price for nothing' and thus starting a bid rumour in the hope that people will view the company as a take-over target and push up the share price.

'for those who like a speculative share' = for those who don't mind losing their money.

'fundamentally cheap' = the shares seem cheap, but who believes the fundamentals?

'neglected for too long' = we've encouraged people to buy these shares before, but few people took any notice.

'the shares should outperform the market' = we think the market will either go down or not move much at all – but these shares should do a bit better than that.

'despite their recent sharp rise' = we didn't predict their recent sharp rise.

'the shares are over-valued' = we didn't recommend them to clients and the shares went up so fast our clients are complaining about it. We weren't at fault (we never are) – other people just keep buying the shares for the wrong reasons. Hopefully, if we say the shares are over-valued, the share price will go down and our clients will stop moaning.

'the shares are under-valued' = why doesn't anyone want to buy the shares? We bought some for our discretionary clients at even higher prices and they are now showing a loss – why won't the share price go back up?

'credibility has not yet been restored' = with a chairman/ management like that, who can believe what they say about future prospects?

'**we are reducing our forecast of profits**' = our earlier forecast was wrong.

'**the management team is excellent**' = that's what their financial PR firm keep saying/the management have just given us a good lunch.

'**highly rated team**' = overpaid team.

'**we have recently visited the company and strongly recommend the shares**' = we were given an excellent tour, all the skeletons were locked in the cupboards, and we had lots of fine wine and good food.

'**the company has ambitious expansion plans**' = the company is likely to have a rights issue so it can buy another company/the company may be paying too much for the companies it takes over.

'**the company has ambitious plans in the States**' = the company paid for our recent first-class trip to the States where we spent two days looking at their operations in the US and the rest of the week was spent wining, dining, lounging by the pool, having a massage, looking up old friends, etc.

'**the company's new drug is to undergo trials**' = they've developed a new drug that might have bad side-effects, or it may be a miracle cure: toss a coin to decide whether or not to buy shares in the company.

'**the company is soon to start drilling/mining in . . .**' = the company hasn't started drilling/mining in that area yet and may not find anything: toss a coin to decide whether or not to buy shares in the company.

'sentiment is mixed' = no one knows what is happening.

'it all depends on the trade figures/economic statistics/ exchange rate' = we don't know what will happen – this is as good an excuse as any if we get it wrong.

'the pound/dollar/Japanese yen should go higher/ lower' = who knows what it will actually do – if we get it wrong, we only said it _should_ go higher/lower, not that it _would_ do that.

Company Chairmen

'barring unforeseen circumstances' = if profits go down it's not _my_ fault, it's due to an unforeseen circumstance.

'the company is doing especially well overseas' = business looks rather flat at home.

'we must try to counter the lack of understanding of our industry' = why don't people appreciate that it's not _my_ fault that the company's profit record is erratic/we will be changing our PR people.

'the current business climate remains uncertain and it is not an easy one in which to operate' = profits are going down, but don't blame me as times are tough.

'the deal looks attractive' = but looks can be deceiving/I don't know for sure if the deal really will prove attractive, but the management keep telling me it's an attractive deal.

'we are delighted to record that our Deputy Chairman/ Chief Executive/Managing Director received a knighthood/CBE/OBE earlier this year' = the company is a regular contributor to the funds of a political party/the company sponsors highbrow arts events in an attempt to appeal to some of the people who make decisions about honours/the person who was honoured spends a lot of company time on government committees sucking up to civil servants.

'despite uninformed comment' = despite the views of people who had the cheek to disagree with my wise words.

'due to circumstances beyond our control' = we were asleep at the time.

'exchange rate difficulties' = we were too stupid to organize our currency transactions/forward pricing/ forward buying properly/we failed to tailor our products to meet overseas needs.

'future prospects look bright' = present prospects are disappointing – hopefully, the future has better things in store.

'this will help the company's standing in the world' = this may not add much to the company's profits, but it will give a boost to my ego.

'I look forward to another satisfactory year' = profits this year look as if they might be much better than last year, but I don't want to say that in case the share price rises sharply before I've bought some more shares in the

company/profits this year look as if they will be much
better than last year – but I don't want to say that in case
there is a sudden downturn in business and I'm proved
wrong.

'I view the future with confidence' = my views may not be
shared by the management of the company, but by
'future' I mean any time within the next twenty years.

'last year we laid the foundations' = last year we didn't
make as much profit as we hope to make this year.

'much depends on . . .' = who knows what will happen?

'our balance sheet remains strong' = profits were
disappointing/profits were down/we made a loss.

'our objective is long-term capital growth' = we were
incapable of making good profits last year.

'problems due to bad weather' = problems due to bad
management who didn't make sufficient provision for
the fact that there might be bad weather.

'problems with production/production difficulties' =
the management couldn't handle the unions/the wrong
sort of machinery was bought and it kept breaking down.

'profits did not materialize' = we fouled up and didn't
make any profits.

'the re-organization and re-structuring are almost complete' = God knows what excuse I'll be able to give next
year if we're still reporting losses/reporting poor profits.

'**results are rather disappointing**' = we fouled up.

'**shareholders should reject the offer for our company. The offer is totally unrealistic**' = they are not offering enough money for the shares/they haven't promised me a job with the company at an enhanced salary if they take us over.

'**I'm sure that shareholders will want to join me in expressing our thanks to the company's staff for all their efforts**' = the staff didn't demand the same salary increase as I received/I hope you will realize that I did more than anyone else and will give me an even warmer 'thanks'.

'**we are taking steps to cope with the new competitive environment**' = we've only just realized it's getting tough out there: maybe we can't cope with it?

'**we thought that after the disappointments of last year**' = we fouled up last year and have now fouled up again.

'**we thought we should rationalize those interests**' = we intend to sell those interests for whatever we can get for them as we can't make a decent profit out of them/the previous management stupidly diversified into areas we don't find particularly attractive and so now we're dumping those diversifications so that we can diversify into something else instead.

'**the company is currently trading ahead of budget**' = the company has a very modest budget/*currently* it is trading ahead of budget, but don't blame me if sales start dropping off next month.

'turnover/trading should be well up on last year' = turnover may go up, but profits might remain fairly static.

'we are very pleased to welcome on our board as a non-executive director' = at last we've found a non-executive director who'll do as he's told/this former civil servant should be able to help us with any problems from Whitehall/he's agreed that one of his companies will give my son a job/he's an old school chum/he might help me get a knighthood.

'the company is well placed to take advantage of any upturn in the economy' = profits are down/the company is performing poorly, but I have to end my report on a positive note/it's not *my* fault the company is performing poorly – blame the government for not stimulating the economy.

Chapter 12:

Twenty-One Brief Basic Reminders

---

1. If you have not already bought shares, then 'practise on paper' first. Choose some shares – but do *not* buy them – follow their progress for three months. This helps you to assess your 'investment temperament' before you risk any real money.

2. Never buy shares from people or companies that are not registered by the appropriate authorities.

3. Remember that shares can go down as well as up. However, buying and selling shares is better than betting on horses: Stock Market dealings are supposed to be regarded as more of an *investment* activity than a gamble.

If you back a horse and you see it performing badly in a race, the bookie who took your bet will not let you withdraw half-way through and give you back some of your money: you have to wait to the end of the race to see if you have lost your entire investment.

If you back a company by buying its shares and you follow its progress via comments in the press, its company reports, the changes in its share price, etc. – and you see that it is unlikely to beat its competitors – then, in most cases, it is highly likely that, if you act in time, you will be able to sell the shares and thus get some of your money back.

4. Remember that successful investing is not only investing in shares that go _up_, but _not_ investing in shares that have a high possibility of going _down_.

5. Make sure your instructions to your broker are always clear and understood.

6. Check that you really do own what you are selling: have there been any scrip issues, share splits, bonus issues, rights issues – are the shares correctly registered?

7. It is often best _not_ to 'put all your eggs in one basket': buying shares in more than one company can help to spread the risk, but be careful your investments are not so widely spread that you never make a worthwhile profit.

8. Remember that a low share price does _not_ necessarily imply that a company's shares are a bargain. The share price may be low because some 'bad news' is expected, and the share price may fall even further.

A 'penny share price' need not mean that the company's Stock Market value is small – the company may have hundreds of millions of shares in issue and be given a 'total value' far higher than a company with a share price in £s, but with far fewer shares in issue.

9. Never rush to buy a share without first finding out something about the company concerned. Most people do not buy a house or car without looking at it first – so why 'invest blind' in shares?

10. Never be afraid to admit mistakes and cut losses on badly performing investments rather than holding on in a vain hope of seeing an improvement. As Edward Phelps once said: 'The man who makes no mistakes does not usually make anything.'

11. Never be too greedy. If a share appears to be greatly over-priced, do not hang on in the hope of getting a few pence more before the share is 'rumbled'. The little bit of extra profit is unlikely to be worth the increased risk. Over-priced shares or markets can sometimes collapse suddenly without much warning.

12. Be patient. If you have shares in a company that is performing well, the management is excellent, and the future looks bright – or if you have bought a share because you strongly believe the company concerned has consider-able take-over potential – then why sell the shares for only a modest (or no) profit, simply out of boredom and wanting to 'do a trade'? This particularly applies if the shares con-cerned are not very speculative and might, in a year or so, go much higher – perhaps as a result of a take-over bid.

Of course, if you have a much better investment 'home' for your money, then that is another matter – but some people sell shares simply because they are bored with them as the share price has dropped slightly or hasn't moved much at all for some time: and then they put the proceeds from the sale into shares in a company that performs even worse!

13. Remember that analysts, chartists, gurus, share tipsters and other experts – and financial website bulletin boards – are sometimes wrong. No one is infallible.

14. Read as widely as possible: several national newspapers (including the *Financial Times* at least every Saturday), a wide variety of magazines, local newspapers – whatever you have time to look at.

Also, don't forget radio and TV programmes: they can offer all sorts of business pointers – not just the financial programmes, but also more general programmes (and even some of the commercials) can lead to companies that might (or might not) have a bright future.

The internet and teletext services are also extremely helpful.

I usually look at the latest financial teletext and website information just before phoning my broker to buy or sell shares – just in case some late financial news may affect my proposed course of action, or provide a pointer to something I should check with my broker.

15. It is often wise not to accept the first take-over offer made for a company – wait and see if a rival, higher, bid is likely, while still bearing in mind the deadlines for acceptance of the bid and the likely prospects for the company's share price if the bid does not succeed.

16. Always take on holidays or trips abroad a list of your shareholdings, plus phone, fax and e-mail details of your stockbroker so that if there is a sudden downturn in the market it will be fairly easy to contact your broker and sell the shares.

17. Personal experience pays. Look around you – at home, at work, on holiday. Maybe you can pick up some pointers towards successful companies or Stock Market trends. Perhaps people are rushing to buy a new product, or you see a lowly-rated company occupying a prime site worth considerably more than its capitalization, or a trend in one country which may soon follow in another: keep your eyes and ears open for investment pointers.

18. Remember the tax situation: ask your broker or financial adviser for advice.

19. Remember that as a shareholder you *own* a part of the company in which you have invested. Look at the company report, company progress, performance of directors, etc. from the viewpoint of one of the company's *owners*.

20. When in doubt – get out. It is better to be safe than sorry. If you have serious doubts about the future of a company in which you have an investment, or you strongly believe a Stock Market Crash is about to happen – then sell your shares.

21. Remember that investing in shares can be fun as well as profitable. However, investing in shares is not a must. There may be times when it is better to keep cash or invest in something other than shares.

Index

RIGHT WAY
PUBLISHING POLICY

HOW WE SELECT TITLES

RIGHT WAY consider carefully every deserving manuscript. Where an author is an authority on his subject but an inexperienced writer, we provide first-class editorial help. The standards we set make sure that every **RIGHT WAY** book is practical, easy to understand, concise, informative and delightful to read. Our specialist artists are skilled at creating simple illustrations which augment the text wherever necessary.

CONSISTENT QUALITY

At every reprint our books are updated where appropriate, giving our authors the opportunity to include new information.

FAST DELIVERY

We sell **RIGHT WAY** books to the best bookshops throughout the world. It may be that your bookseller has run out of stock of a particular title. If so, he can order more from us at any time – we have a fine reputation for "same day" despatch, and we supply any order, however small (even a single copy), to any bookseller who has an account with us. We prefer you to buy from your bookseller, as this reminds him of the strong underlying public demand for **RIGHT WAY** books. However, you can order direct from us by post, by phone with a credit card, or through our web site.

FREE

If you would like an up-to-date list of all **RIGHT WAY** and **RIGHT WAY PLUS** titles currently available, please send a stamped self-addressed envelope to:

ELLIOT RIGHT WAY BOOKS, BRIGHTON ROAD, LOWER KINGSWOOD, TADWORTH, SURREY, KT20 6TD, U.K. or visit our web site at www.right-way.co.uk